EVENING GARDENS

EVENING GARDENS

*Planning & planting a landscape to dazzle
the senses after sundown*

By Cathy Wilkinson Barash

PRINCIPAL PHOTOGRAPHERS

CATHY WIILKINSON BARASH

DEREK FELL

ILLUSTRATIONS

JEAN CARLSON MASSEAU

CHAPTERS™

CHAPTERS PUBLISHING LTD. SHELBURNE, VERMONT 05482

To all evening gardeners—
the night life is for you.

Published by
Chapters Publishing Ltd.
2031 Shelburne Road, Shelburne, Vermont 05482

Library of Congress Cataloguing-in-Publication Data

Barash , Cathy Wilkinson
Evening gardens : planning & planting a landscape to dazzle the senses
    after sundown / by Cathy Wilkinson Barash.
        p.   cm.
    Includes bibliographical references and index.
    ISBN 1-881527-14-X : $29.95. — ISBN 1-881527-13-1 : $19.95
    1. Night gardens.   2. Plants, Ornamental.   3. Landscape gardening.
    I. Title.
    SB433.6.B37   1993
    635.9'67—dc20   93-7631
                                                              CIP

Trade distribution by
Firefly Books Ltd.
250 Sparks Avenue, Willowdale, Ontario
Canada M2H 2S4

Printed and bound in Canada by
Friesen Printers, Altona, Manitoba

Designed by Hans Teensma / Impress, Inc., Northampton, Massachusetts
Art Director: Dominique Pratt

Cover photograph:
Night-blooming cereus (*Hylocereus undatus*) by Derek Fell

Contents

ACKNOWLEDGMENTS... 9

FOREWORD 11

INTRODUCTION 12

1. A GARDEN FOR EVENING ENJOYMENT 17

2. EVENING GARDEN ARCHITECTURE 23

3. PLANTS FOR THE EVENING GARDEN 31

Sculpture & Silhouette 36

Textured Bark 56

Flowers Aglow at Sunset 61

Bright Flowers 69

Pale Flowers on the Ground 77

White Flowers 81

Night Bloomers 94

Silver Foliage 108

Foliage for Contrast 113

Fragrant Plants 122

Stars of the Evening Garden 133

4. LIGHTING... 147

5. PLANS FOR YOUR EVENING GARDEN 157

APPENDICES

Sources & Further Reading.................................... 164

Zone Map 170

Photography Credits 172

Index 173

Acknowledgments

Thanks to all those people who helped create this book.

Technical Help: Toro; Intermatic; Nightscaping; Hadco; Doug at Xyquest; Betsy Bibla of Night Lights in Huntington, New York; and Bill Switzek of Torrance, California.

Photographic Assists: Dency Kane; Susanne Lucas; Carole Ottesen; Liz Ball; Michael Dodge; John Minet; John Trager of The Huntington Library; Kathy Tilley of Callaway Gardens in Pine Mountain, Georgia; Bonnie Burton of Butchart Gardens in British Columbia, Canada; and Colvin Randall of Longwood Gardens in Kennett Square, Pennsylvania.

Great Gardens, Plants & Designs: Darrel Trout; David Dobbins; Bob Titus; Carole Ottesen; Rosalind Creasy; Charles Cresson; Georgene McKim; Camilla Christ & Scott Bell; Tim Mawson; Jim Wilson; Patricia Lanza; Susan and Jay Kuhlman; Betty Pruehsner; Shirley Kerins; Steven Frowine of White Flower Farm in Litchfield, Connecticut; Pat Slator of Old Westbury Gardens in Old Westbury, New York; Janine Adams and Bill Welch at the Missouri Botanical Garden; Wendy Lynne Fehse; Anthony J. Mannino; and Richard A. Waldman.

All the others who helped me create this book: Agent extraordinaire Kit Ward; my untiring editor Barry Estabrook; West Coast folks Toodie and Vern Walt; and Mark Sink of the James L. Breese estate.

And those who kept things together on the home front: My generous landlady Rizz Arthur Dean; everhelpful Bill Barash; David Corrody; Brendan Earls; and especially my cat Sebastian.

With their help and the help of others I have undoubtedly forgotten to mention, this book has come together in a way that would have been impossible had I done it alone.

Page 2: Daylily (Hemerocallis 'Goddess')
Page 5: Angel's trumpet (Brugmansia 'Charles Grimaldi')
Page 6: Ribbon grass (Phalaris arundinacea picta)
Page 8: Bob Titus's Rose Garden at dusk

Foreword

CATHY WILKINSON BARASH has the nuts-and-bolts expertise of a horticultural technician, the eye of an artist and the ability of a natural writer to describe plants and settings accurately and vividly. Most of all, she loves life and lets it show.

Evening Gardens will be especially valuable to busy gardeners who barely return home from work before the sun sets. It will also be useful to southern and western gardeners who try to avoid the sweltering outdoors until after sundown.

Two of the most important developments during my nearly 50 years of gardening have been the resurgence of interest in water gardening and the introduction of safe, handsome, low-voltage lighting for gardens.

Cathy understands the significance of these trends: Pools and fountains are like magnets in gardens, and unobtrusive garden lighting guides our footsteps as we explore the landscape.

She understands how flowers seem to change color and shrubs and trees take on new shapes, first at dusk and again when we throw the switch on the garden lights.

She understands the need for structures in the garden—walls, gates, arbors, pergolas, steps and terraces—especially during the morning and evening hours when the lengthening and diminishing shadows reshape gardens.

Every garden should have a stone bench or an Adirondack chair tucked away, walled in by shrubs or vines. And every gardener should find a little time to retreat to his or her own mini-sanctuary to listen to the night noises, to revel in the fragrance of an old-fashioned tall white nicotiana and to let the kinship of humankind and plants heal his or her care-battered soul.

Pink calla lilies, **above.**
Opposite: *Moonflowers bloom only at night.*

It's not easy to describe the special charm of after-hours gardens, but Cathy does it so compellingly that you will think seriously about changing your routine.

After all, how else can you expect to enjoy an evening primrose, a night-blooming cereus, a moonflower or a tuberose?

—Jim Wilson

Introduction

❧

MY INTEREST IN evening gardening has evolved over time. For 12 years, I was employed at a local arboretum and had somewhat normal work hours. At the end of my day, I enjoyed coming home, changing into comfortable clothes, brewing a pot of herbal tea and, when weather permitted, sitting on a small bench on the patio and gazing into the garden and through the woods to the harbor below. This was my own time to unwind from the pressures of the day and let the beauty of the garden quiet my mind.

The scenes from my days off were not nearly so bucolic. Even though I am basically a lazy gardener and employ as many time- and energy-saving methods as I can—mulching, interplanting and trying to use plants that require little maintenance—the garden still demanded some of my time and energy.

The way I garden, a lot of hours are spent in the garden in spring—cleaning it out, removing protective mulch, moving existing plantings, starting seeds, planting and mulching. Although I promise each year to pace myself, I end up spending three or four 10-hour days in the garden. I am thankful when the sun goes down and I can retreat into the house and sink into a hot tub.

The first inkling of planning a garden specifically for evening enjoyment came one languid summer evening. I arrived home from a new job tired and cranky, an hour later than usual. I slammed my car door—a signal for my husband to turn on the outdoor lights—but there was no response.

As I walked toward the door, I tripped on one of the flagstones and fell. I felt defeated and depressed that life was passing me by as I worked many long hours. As I got up, I was aware of a sweet aroma in the air. A light was on in the bedroom, shedding a pale glow outside. I looked up to see large, luminescent white moonflowers seemingly floating on the air surrounding the bedroom window. Upon closer examination, I realized they were part of two vines that had been planted on either side of the window.

On my next day off, I decided to photograph the moonflowers and was there to

Shirley poppy, **above.** *White and purple flowers come to life as the light fades,* **opposite.**

watch the very slow geometric progression from bud to fully opened flower. Although the process took about half an hour, I was captivated and found that sitting quietly watching the flowers slowly open was like meditating.

I began to create gardens for evening enjoyment from that point on. Moonflowers were joined by such night-fragrant plants as nicotiana and tuberose, which, with their white flowers, were also visible in the dim light of the patio at night. By August, the garden was more fragrant and just as beautiful at night as it was during the day.

Hymenocallis narcissiflora, or basket flowers, shimmer in the moonlight.

One night, I came upstairs from the basement where I was working and chanced a peek outside. The garden seemed alive, shimmering in the light of the full moon. What a delight! My Japanese maple was beautifully silhouetted, the dwarf conifers were glistening with dew and the hakonechloa virtually glowed.

As I became aware of my need for a garden to enjoy at night, my interests shifted. Suddenly, I paid attention to the multitude of plants that have variegated leaves. I noticed that when the light fades, the cream-colored edges of a particular hosta show up well, while the solid green-leaved hosta that is equally attractive in the daytime is virtually invisible.

I moved the green-leaved hosta to another garden that is distant from the house and not viewed at night. I put white snowdrops near the entrance so I could look at them both day and night. I included some plants that I thought would be perfect for the evening garden, like light- and bright-colored asters and snow-white boltonia. However, I soon realized that they tightly closed their flowers at night, and thus were only interesting in the daytime. Although tulips and crocuses close at night, too, their outer petals are still visible after sundown—so I planted more of them in the evening garden.

I must admit that I use "evening" in the broadest sense possible, to include any time from late afternoon to the dead of night. All these times are magical to me.

In the late afternoon, as the rays of the sun lengthen, the light is warm and mellow, making yellows, reds and oranges stand out. As the light fades, some of the cooler colors—fuchsia and some blues, pinks and purples—come to life and almost fluoresce.

Later, dark colors melt into the gloom—reds and purples disappear, as do the green leaves. Pale and light colors, especially white, remain visible even in the dimmest light. In darkness, the light portions of variegated leaves seem to float; white flowers appear stalkless and seem to hover above the ground.

When I was out and about in the evening, I started to look around with a keen eye, taking note of the plants that caught my eye. I soon realized that other elements besides the plants were grabbing my attention. The background of the garden, what professionals call "hardscape," played an important role, too. White and light-colored walls, paths, trellises and other man-made elements stood out.

As the holiday season rolled around, the final element of an evening garden made itself apparent. Holiday lights were everywhere. What a waste, it seemed to me, the inveterate lazy gardener, that people spend so much time and effort to put up lights in the trees for only a couple of weeks of pleasure. Why not leave some of the lights up year-round? I'm not talking about Santa and his sleigh on the roof, but a few small white lights that highlight the trees and fences.

I have made a pointed effort to experience the garden as much as possible at night. When the weather is cold or inclement, I can sit at the dining room table and gaze out into the garden. I enjoy the shape of the Japanese maple accented with a dusting of snow in winter, the large, nodding, bell-shaped guinea hen flowers in spring, the profusion of flowers of

Dark foliage contrasts with white furniture, flowers and house to make this garden as spectacular at night as during the day.

all shapes and sizes in summer and the cushions of chrysanthemums in autumn.

At other times, I sit outside in the dark with the lights off and focus on the fragrances—the lemony scent of the winter honeysuckle in late winter, the sweetness of the daffodils in spring, the perfumes of nicotiana, tuberose and moonflowers in summer and the slight pungency of chrysanthemums in autumn.

The sounds of the garden at night are equally enchanting—the rustling of a breeze blowing through the ornamental grasses and the whooshing sound the wind makes as it travels through the tall pines.

One of the advantages of being in the garden at night is the darkness itself. We humans cannot see well at night, so we are forced to slow down and can take time to identify sights, sounds and scents. We are unable to see the weeds, so guilt does not drive us to work in the garden. Instead, we can enjoy it.

In the heat of summer, the garden is very sensual at night—warm fragrant air caresses bare skin while fireflies glimmer and dance their mating dance. At night you cannot be easily seen, so you can wear as little or as much as you wish.

One of my great pleasures is skinny-dipping by the light of the full moon in late May or early June. As I stroke toward the deep end of the pool, I can see the brightness of the flowers of Daphne 'Carol Mackie.' When I come up for air, I gulp in their sweet perfume and feel united with my garden.

Night falls upon us all, so consider creating your own garden for evening enjoyment. By combining plant material, lighting and design, you can enjoy your garden as I do mine—any time of night or day.

—*Cathy Wilkinson Barash*

CHAPTER I

A Garden for Evening Enjoyment

ᘔ

OW MANY OF YOU have endless daylight hours to while away sitting in the garden? With a garden planned for evening enjoyment, you will have more time to enjoy the fruits of your labor. Not only is this type of garden attractive during the day, but it comes into its glory as the light begins to fade. Brightly colored flowers, like black-eyed susans and cardinal flowers, glow in the warm light of the late afternoon. A bit later, pale and cool-colored flowers, like isotoma and cineraria, reflect the early evening light and begin to fluoresce.

As darkness descends, plants with light-colored variegations in their leaves stand out, while their deep green-leaved cousins become virtually invisible. White and pale-colored flowers, like autumn clematis, sweet alyssum and candytuft, are visible even in the dimmest light and seem to pop out of the landscape under a full moon.

Creating a garden for evening enjoyment can be as simple as adding one or two plants to an existing garden or as complex as creating an entirely new garden in one season. But transformation need not mean complete renovation. In-deed, it is often more successful when done over a period of time rather than as an instant makeover.

Take a judicious look at your garden in the evening. Which plants work in the scheme of an evening garden? Not every plant needs to be an evening plant, but there should be enough to provide interest. Start by winnowing out plants that are neither superlative daytime plants nor an asset to the evening garden. Transplant them to another area or give them away. Then you can look at the blank spaces you've created and decide which evening stars to add.

Above: *A Cereus dayamii. Tropical waterlilies scent the evening garden,* **opposite.**

The Elements

*With its border of white spring flowers, this garden path, **below**, is also inviting at night. **Opposite:** Night-scented stock is head and shoulders above its daytime relative when it comes to fragrance.*

I N DESIGNING an evening garden, remember that you are creating an illusion. The three vital elements are the hardscape, plant material and lighting.

The **hardscape** is the first design element to consider when creating a truly lovely evening garden. The hardscape comprises all the architectural features upon which the garden is built—walls, trellises, paths, borders, arbors, pergolas and fences. I also consider any water elements—

ponds, pools, streams, waterfalls and fountains—to be a part of the hardscape as well as the finishing touches, such as ornamentation.

The second element to consider, and by far the most important, is the **plant material**. Any white flowers are visible by moonlight. Yet de-

pending on the viewing time, other colors do amazing things as daylight fades. The pale purple of sage and the blues, mauves and magentas of cineraria almost fluoresce in the waning light. The late-afternoon sun brings a warm glow to red salvias and orange lily flowers. Dark colors, like the deep purple of *Clematis* x *jackmanii*, however, all but disappear with the setting sun.

Plants with variegated foliage, like white-tipped hemlock or variegated lilyturf, are also visually interesting in an evening garden. While the green portion of the foliage almost disappears with the waning light, the lighter variegation is visible at night and adds to the illusion of the garden as a collection of floating elements.

Plant material in an evening garden needs to be well mixed to make the evening garden a year-round treat. Try small snowdrops and crocuses for the late winter garden, perfumed climbing moonflowers for the late summer and autumn garden and *Sasa veitchii*, a bamboo with evergreen leaves whose edges fade to buff in fall, for the late autumn and winter garden.

Scent plays an important role in the evening garden, too. The true stars of an evening garden are the plants that either bloom only at night, like four o'clocks and daturas, or are fragrant only at night, like nicotianas. Remember Mother Nature's role in the scheme of things: The perfume that fills the night air was not intended for human enjoyment, but rather to attract nocturnal pollinators, such as moths and

bats, to the plants.

Lighting, whether natural or artificial, can play a significant role in the evening garden. Not only can it

be used to highlight plants, but it can also be positioned to cast interesting shadows. Artificial lighting can illuminate the entire garden, spotlight areas of interest or be so subtle as to recreate the light of a full moon. But you don't need artificial lighting to enjoy an evening garden. Many moments I cherish in my evening garden are by the light of the moon.

If you do decide to light your garden, it's best to take things one step at a time. Technological advances allow a wide range of lighting effects that you can create without having to hire an electrician.

Certain plants can be spotlighted, others may have branches wrapped with tiny lights. Pathways can be illuminated directly or indirectly with any number of devices.

There are dozens of fixtures, dimmers and filters that allow for the optimal volume and intensity of light in each garden—controlling the interplay of light and shadow and helping to create the desired mood.

When I first introduced lighting to my garden, I placed one spotlight at the base of the oaks in the backyard, aimed upward into the branches. After viewing it that way for several months, I felt the look was too harsh, so I aimed two lower-wattage spotlights to gently graze the bark with their light, showing off the strength of the tree.

In my main garden, I have worked gradually, first illuminating the edge of the garden with small low-voltage lights. I then added a floodlight to my Japanese maple and even challenged my husband to wrap each branch of the tree with small white Christmas lights, but he has thus far declined. As my garden grows and changes, so will the lighting plan.

Creating the Garden

WHEN PLANNING an evening garden, try to think carefully about its placement. It should be in an area that you can easily see. The buzz word for an evening garden is enjoyment. It should be easily accessible—you don't want to have to trek through muck and mire to view your creation, no matter how splendiferous it is.

Consider creating several small areas of evening interest instead of one large one—perhaps a small plot along the driveway for when you arrive home or a patch outside a room where you spend time in the evening.

A spring-flowering viburnum shrub would nicely offset a planting of tulips in an evening garden. They, in turn, could be followed by silvery lavender cotton and some fragrant summer-blooming bulbs, like tuberose and summer hyacinth. Cleome placed behind the bulbs would show off spidery flowers throughout the summer. Some bright white alyssum would light up the walkway to the house. Intersperse some heliotrope for fantastic summer fragrance. Add one or two dwarf conifers, especially the types with variegated or yellow needles and you are set for year-round interest.

I cannot emphasize enough the importance of locating the evening garden in an area where it can be experienced from indoors as well as out. One of the most impressive evening gardens I have seen was sited so that the house formed three walls of the garden. Plants were chosen that visually enhanced the garden even when the weather might be too chilly to venture outside. Early spring bulbs were important to ease the transition from the snowy whiteness of winter to the white and green of the garden in midsummer.

I can look out onto one of my gardens from my sun room/dining room. In earliest spring, I have large clusters of snowdrops near the low-to-the-ground tier lights. As the season progresses, more and more plants come out of their dormancy. The white flowers of the flowering tobacco stand out like little stars high above the foliage.

From midsummer until killing frost, the moonflowers are outstanding. Trained on tall tomato stakes, they grow up between four large windows. I can watch them open in early evening and drink in their beauty and fragrance throughout the night.

I plan for viewing the garden in autumn—chrysanthemums, dahlias and Japanese anemones, all with pale or white flowers, shine back at me. Once all the leaves have fallen and the garden has been put to bed, the architectural plants come into their own for the winter. My Japanese maple has such wonderful form, whether illuminated by the setting sun, the moon or artificial lighting.

You may even get a sense of the finished garden before you start. On a comfortable night with a full moon, go out to where you plan to site the garden and observe the area for 15 or 20 minutes. Do the same thing from the inside viewing area.

A garden for evening enjoyment can be a private space for you alone to treasure or an area to share with family and friends. Unlike typical gardens, the garden planned for evening viewing can be enjoyed any time of day or night.

Daffodils, **below,** *should form the basis of the early-spring evening garden.* **Opposite:** *Magnolia grandiflora.*

Evening Garden Architecture

I THINK OF THE HARDSCAPE as the backbone upon which the garden is built. Basically, it encompasses all the nonliving components, except for the lighting: walls, trellises, fences, gates, arbors, pergolas, gazebos, paths, walkways, water elements and ornamentation. An evening gardener must look at each component with a different eye from the daytime gardener. In an evening garden, color has a tremendous impact on the ultimate appearance. Obviously, white is most visible at night and can be seen even without the light of a full moon. Clear bright colors, such as pinks and yellows, stand out in the late afternoon, but pale as the light dims. Reds disappear almost completely, while dark colors fade into the gloom.

Walls & Trellises

IN THE EVENING GARDEN, a white or light color usually works best as a background. Even without additional lighting, a plant's outline can usually be seen against a light-colored backdrop.

A white wall also works well with various lighting techniques. Aim a spotlight up at a large tree or shrub that is in front of a white wall—interesting shadows will be projected onto the wall. By varying the height and angle of the light, you can alter the shadow's shape.

Place a spotlight between a plant and a wall and aim it toward the wall to create a dramatic silhouette. This works especially well with plants that have interesting forms, such as yuccas with their sharp swordlike leaves, and small deciduous trees that have unique leafless forms in winter, such as Japanese maples.

Keep in mind that, for anything to

White-painted arbors, **above,** *and gates,* **opposite,** *stand out in the evening.*

The white fence, gate and arbor will show up well at night, making a striking border at the Missouri Botanical Garden.

show up in an evening garden, you must contrast light and dark elements. No lighting technique can help bring out the forms of dark green plants backed by a dark wall.

Some walls can be painted white or a pale color, but with others there is no option. Assume that the garden abuts the side of a dark brown house. How can the hardscape be adapted for an evening garden without repainting the house? A simple solution is to erect a white or natural wood trellis 6 to 12 inches from the house. The contrast between the light tone of the trellis and the darkness of the space behind adds a sense of depth. Leave enough of the trellis empty so that you don't lose its intended purpose.

Another possible solution is to plant light-colored plants or those with variegated foliage around the foundation. A canoe birch, with its white bark, shows up well against a dark wall at night. Lighting the tree from below accentuates the contrast of the light bark against the dark house.

The use of silver foliage plants, such as some of the larger artemisias, provides a striking counterpoint to a dark wall. A subtle spotlight with a pale blue hue makes silver plants shimmer as if they are lit by the light of the moon. Another good evening foil for a dark wall is to train a white-flowering vine, like clematis or moonflowers, on a string or wire up the wall.

Fences & Gates

THE STYLE AND COLOR of a fence can help set the tone of a garden. A dark fence will disappear in the evening gloom, so that a vine trained on it, like honeysuckle, will appear to float in the darkness. A low white picket fence conjures up images of a cottage garden and is visible into the evening. Bamboo, split and bent to form U shapes, makes a simplistic low barrier for a Japanese-influenced garden and is usually of a light enough color to be seen at night.

Depending on its form and function, you may not want to feature your fence at night. For example, a metal deer fence acts as a security barrier between hungry deer and the delicious plants in the garden. It is functional but unattractive during the day. At night, however, it is virtually invisible, so that once in the spell of the garden, you are unaware of any man-made boundaries.

Consider the numerous styles of gates to help set a mood. For example, a white picket fence need not have a plain white picket gate. The gate might be ornate—a sort of gingerbread effect—or it might support an arbor arching above it.

Arbors & Pergolas

AN ARBOR, by definition, is a tunnel-like passage shaded by vines growing up latticework on either side. A pergola is also an arbor, but it has an open roof of cross rafters or latticework supported on posts or columns, usually with climbing vines.

The difference between the two is the placement of the latticework. The latticework forms the sides of an arbor; the pergola has columns or posts that support a latticework roof.

An arbor is most impressive in the evening garden when covered with plants that have abundant foliage and flowers along the stems or vines, such as roses, moonflowers or honeysuckle. A pergola is often covered with a plant that has a long stem and a heavy vining habit, such as a fra-

Roses climb a white-painted pergola at the Huntington Library in California.

grant white or pale purple wisteria.

Arbors and pergolas are attractive focal points in a garden. If painted white, the structure itself becomes important, but if painted green or brown, the structure will be less visible in the evening and the plants will appear to be climbing on their own.

A friend has a marvelous rose garden with several arbors. It is a wonderful evening garden, although that was not his intent. On the white arbors, he has trained dark-colored roses. At night, you see the shape of the arbors, with the sense that something dark is twisting around them. On the dark green arbors, he has trained white roses. At night, you lose the sense of the arbors—arches of fragrant white roses seem to float in the middle of the garden.

A gazebo, **above,** *can be a superb vantage point from which to view the evening garden.* **Opposite:** *Light-colored stepping stones make this path visible at night.*

Gazebos

A GAZEBO IS A fun structure to include if you have a large enough garden. Depending on its design, you may have moonflower vines or, in the warmer South and West, jasmine vines climbing up the gazebo sides, either on supports or on the latticework. A gazebo has a solid roof that provides protection so you can enjoy your garden in the rain or mist without discomfort.

A gazebo is much more than a focal point in a garden. It is a superb vantage point from which you can view the rest of the garden. It is a place where you can sit quietly on a moonless summer night and watch the lightning bugs skim through the garden. It can be a place for entertaining—the setting for romantic dinners for two or cocktails for eight—and a sanctuary for witnessing a thunderstorm.

One of the most romantic gazebos I have seen was in British Columbia. It was set at the edge of the garden, so you could see its white form from a distance at night. The side of the gazebo that faced the house was completely trellised, ensuring privacy and creating a perfect milieu for a collection of clematis to clamber. From within, I looked out toward the pasture and orchards where I saw deer feeding. What made it really special was a hot tub set in the center. It was a romantic vantage point from which to enjoy the garden at night.

A gazebo is normally a minimum of 10 feet in diameter. Anything smaller will prove crowded and almost preclude entertaining. In areas where bugs are a problem, consider having the gazebo screened in or have roll-up mosquito netting to cover the openings.

If desired, uplight the gazebo, either from a distance or up close. Be sure to view the lighting from within the gazebo before it is permanently installed. What might look beautiful from a distance might actually create tremendous glare for those seated inside.

Take special care when choosing plants that will surround and climb the gazebo. Include a night-blooming vine like moonflower for both its majestic flowers and its heavenly fragrance. Don't include more than a few fragrant plants, as the scents may clash with each other.

Paths & Walkways

A PATH THROUGH an evening garden makes the garden more intimate—it makes the stroller feel a part of the garden, rather than like an outsider looking in.

The material you choose for your path helps set the tone of the evening garden. A simple path that is nothing more than packed soil is very naturalistic during the day, but needs lighting to make it visible at night, even if it is covered with a mulch of shredded leaves, wood bark or pine needles.

Stones of all shapes, sizes and col-

Brick paths are perhaps the most formal walkways and may require lighting at night.

ors can be used to create a walkway. A white sand path winding through a cactus or succulent garden is striking and has a mystical look in the moonlight. A naturalistic area at the Missouri Botanical Garden has white stepping stones that, especially in the light of the moon, invite you to step off the main path and follow them further into the garden.

To create a similar effect in a woodland garden, use light-colored gravel. Dry Japanese gardens, with their use of gravel and sand, make exquisite evening gardens. An interesting combination can be achieved using a light gravel pathway with large dark-colored stepping stones—the effect is almost three-dimensional at night. If the stepping stones are very dark, the visual illusion is that you are stepping into a hole rather than onto solid ground.

Poured concrete is another option for a walkway. Instead of having regular rectangles of concrete like a sidewalk, make the edges irregular so it looks like stone. Another variation

is to embed small stones or gravel in the surface of the concrete to make it look like a stone walkway, but with the added stability of concrete. White stones embedded in concrete will glimmer in the evening garden.

A brick path is perhaps the most formal looking walkway of all, especially when you get involved in different designs. If you don't want the walkway to appear brand new, consider purchasing used brick—it will contribute a look of distinction to the path.

Bricks are available in a range of shades, depending on how they are manufactured. The typical red bricks need lighting to make them visible in the evening garden. If you use white bricks, however, you might not need additional lighting.

Use lighting to create a mood and act as a guide along the walkway. Incorporate path lighting—soft, low lights that illuminate an area below and around them.

No matter what material and lighting scheme you decide upon,

design your path so that it curves through the garden. A garden path is made for strolling slowly and for frequent pauses to admire the plants. A zigzag path can be laid out to bring you right up to a special plant or an interesting vista.

A well-placed bench or seat encourages strollers to stop and rest. A white bench that is softly lighted from above to simulate the look of moonlight will show up well in a garden. Even a bowing out or widening of one side of the path is a suggestion to move over and explore the area a bit closer. If the main path is bluestone, a white gravel path around a tree invites the walker to examine the bark close up.

Water

WATER IS A FANCIFUL element to add to an evening garden, whether it is in the form of a large pool, a small pond, a fountain or even a bird bath. Water will also attract wildlife to the garden.

In the late afternoon, you can watch all sorts of creatures stop by for a drink—a wide array of birds, squirrels and the occasional neighborhood cat or dog. I sometimes see the local wild fox in early evening—he tends to gravitate to the bird bath near the front of the house.

At night, water is black and mysterious unless it is illuminated. A pool or pond can be lit from below the surface, but do this only if the water is crystal clear—murky water is singularly unattractive when lit.

Water can also be used as a mirror to catch reflections of other lighted objects, but only if it is still—movement spoils the reflection.

A fountain, stream or waterfall adds the melodious noises of water to the evening landscape. Lighting the source draws attention to the trickling or rushing sounds.

Depending on the scene you are trying to create, you may make the lighting subtle or add drama with color. At Butchart Gardens in British Columbia, the overall effect is flamboyant. Yellow, red and green lights shine up into a Japanese maple that is, in turn, reflected in a pond.

You may not want to create such a dramatic look at home, so experiment with the many lighting options. Look upon your evening garden and the use of lights as an artistic creation—not everyone has the same taste.

ural as a well-placed white rock or even a well-worn piece of white driftwood sticking out of some greenery.

Containers are excellent for adding that special final touch. A friend has a wonderful white clay pot fashioned in the shape of Medusa's head. What impressed me was the vision of this head staring at us as we walked through the garden after sundown.

Another friend has a bonsai garden planted underneath a Japanese maple. Atop the miniature fence that surrounds the garden, he has placed various crystals. It is especially mystical when the light of the full moon is reflected on all facets of the stones.

Moderation is the key to creating an evening garden that is neither garish nor gaudy. Ornamentation should enhance the garden without being ostentatious.

Whether large or small (from a life-sized Greek goddess to minia-

ture tortoises), any ornamentation should contrast enough with its background so that it is noticed at night. Try angling a spotlight down from above so that the light barely grazes the surface of the ornament.

Don't forget to include a piece of furniture or two. On a trip to Georgia, I saw an old-fashioned swing mounted in a small pergola—all painted white, of course. How delightful to sway in the breeze surrounded by moonflowers.

White wrought-iron furniture adds an elegant, visible touch to the evening garden. However, you may prefer that the furniture blend into the background. An arborist friend has carved out several old logs to create wooden chairs and a sofa.

Whatever you decide, just make sure you have an outdoor vantage point from which you can comfortably enjoy your creation.

Ornamentation

FOR ME, THE FINAL touch in the hardscape is ornamentation. This may conjure up visions of everything from an ornate garden complete with topiary and marble statuary to little concrete elves on suburban lawns.

For the sake of your garden, try to overcome these prejudices. Ornamentation can be as simple and nat-

A well-placed, white-painted bench encourages evening strollers to stop and rest.

CHAPTER 3

Plants for the Evening Garden

IF YOU ARE NOT artistically inclined, choosing color for the garden can be a perplexing task. Although countless books have been written on the topic, many gardeners still ask themselves whether or not they can place purple flowers next to pinks, yellows by reds. If the idea of balancing colors—employing a color wheel to determine the placement and colors of plants and other elements—is intimidating, you can breathe a sigh of

relief. Contrary to its importance in planning a daytime garden, color plays a relatively insignificant role in the plan of an evening garden.

Walk outside and look at an existing garden in the dark. Get a good distance from the house so that street lights and indoor lights are not illuminating the landscape. At first, after leaving the brightness of the house, you may find yourself temporarily blind. After a few minutes, your eyes will begin to adjust, but what you'll see is virtually a black-and-white world. This is normal night vision. In low light levels, only the rods, the black-and-white receptors in the eye, are active. The cones, sensitive to colors, are inactive in low light.

It is interesting to observe the garden

as the daylight dims and finally fades into darkness. As I walk around my garden in the late afternoon, the bright, warm colors glow in the slowly diminishing light. My sister-in-law has cardinal flowers planted at the edge of a woodland, facing west. The brilliant red flowers seem to catch fire in the late afternoon. Even the most common red geranium takes on a special glow in early evening.

Above: *The versatile clematis.*
Opposite: *A strikingly elegant datura.*

One of the most awesome sights I have come upon was when driving in southern Portugal. As I came around the side of a hill, a golden valley was laid out before

next to their brightly colored companions came into their own.

That's one of the reasons I love clematis in the garden. With such a range of varieties and colors that bloom over a long period of time, they brighten the garden any time of day. Some of the purple (like *C.* x *jackmanii*) and fuchsia (*C.* 'Ernest Markham') flowering varieties take on a life of their own in the late afternoon.

Pale yellow flowers, like coreopsis 'Moonbeam' and cowslips, stay vibrant in the fading light, while the green leaves and stems that are visible all day begin to fade and blend into the deepening gloom.

On a moonless night, without additional lighting, the large rhododendrons and hemlocks that provide a backdrop for part of my garden completely disappear. However, the shiny leaves of the holly reflect any ambient light, and the variegated plants, such as variegated ivy, come into their own. All those lovely light-colored variegations pop out, while the deep green background fades in the dim light.

I once visited a garden with 20 or more different hostas. Looking at it at night was like a brainteaser, trying to discern whether the bold, visible variegations were at the edges of small leaves or at the center of large leaves. This garden had a wonderful otherworldly quality. White and pale-colored flowers seemed to

me—it was almost blinding in the late-afternoon sun. As I got closer, I saw that it was an enormous field of sunflowers, planted so close together that all I could see were the golden yellow petals. Even the token sunflowers in my garden are brilliant in the late afternoon, vividly reminding me of my Portuguese visit.

Calendulas and marigolds, with their marvelous hues of orange and yellow, were prominent in my edible-flower garden last year. Late one

afternoon, I went out to pick some flowers and realized I could not just label a garden for one use. Here were these beautiful flowers glowing at the end of the day, showing their versatility. Suddenly, my edible-flower garden took on another dimension—it had fantastic evening possibilities as well.

As the light faded, the reds and oranges began to lose a bit of their glory. However, some of the blues, pinks, purples and violets that paled by day

Evening Gardens

float in the air and glow in the moonlight. White cosmos were eye-catching—visible 2 or 3 feet above ground level, atop their invisible feathery foliage.

The twisted and gnarled shape of Harry Lauder's walking stick was even more evident silhouetted against a white wall than it was in full sunlight. Porcupine grass was noticeable, not only for the bright striations of its leaves and its tall dignified form, but also for the soft sounds of the breeze rustling through its leaves.

The true delight of an evening garden comes as darkness falls and the night-blooming flowers open. Watch any of the night-blooming cacti slowly bloom and you will be witness to one of nature's wonders. The swollen bud gradually expands, revealing a magnificent and complex flower within—its delicate beauty is a great contrast to the spiny plant from which it arises.

Other nocturnal flowers perfume the air, sending olfactory messages to their pollinators. Flowering tobacco, with its starlike blossoms, emits a delightfully sweet fragrance only at night, calling to the moths that continue nature's cycle: In exchange for a drink of nectar, the moths transfer pollen from one plant to another.

When the moon rises and bathes the garden in its cool light, it creates a new view and mood. Just by choosing the right plants for the right space and time, a completely natural and changing scenario will be enacted night after night.

Seeing Old Friends in a New Light

ONE OF THE KEYS to being a successful evening gardener is to look at old garden friends with a keener eye—one tuned to night interest. As I looked outside one evening last winter, the snow and ice had begun to recede. Although by day there seemed to be a paucity of plant material and everything looked sodden and dreary, by night there were many gems that caught my eye.

The melting snow revealed the early spring bulbs just surfacing. Although the crocuses were closed for the night, the flowers were visible as small white and pale blue buds dap-pled with moonlight. The graceful, white, nodding flowers of the snow-drops, planted in a large mass near the edge of the garden, shone in the moonlight. The silver leaves of the dusty miller that survived the winter appeared luminescent. The sword-like leaves of the yucca were formidable in silhouette. The leafless form of the Japanese maple was accented with lighting at its base, which showed off its timeless beauty.

A tremendous diversity of plant material can be used in an evening garden. Some flowers only bloom at night, and they deserve a special place in every evening garden. None should be without the vining moonflower, climbing up a trellis, an arbor or even a string, with its beautiful white flowers that open in the evening. Even

without a pond, a night-blooming waterlily can be grown in a lined whiskey barrel, adding to the enchantment of the garden.

Conversely, some of the joys of the daytime garden, like Greek windflowers, asters and boltonia, close up completely at night and become inconspicuous. If there is nothing else to recommend the plant, consider moving it to another area. Although not every plant in the garden has to be a nighttime star, you may not want too many areas that look blacked out.

Choose plants for their shape and the architecture they provide off-season. The *Franklinia* tree has lovely white flowers late in the summer; in winter, the sinewy form of its branches is an asset when lighted at night. During the growing season, the leaves of the snake-bark maples are striking, while in winter, especially at night, the white striations of the bark are remarkable.

Plants such as hostas and New Guinea impatiens may be included for their foliage, which is of interest for a longer period than their flowers. Even consider edibles, from the palest green kohlrabi, with its unique round form sitting on top of the soil, to yellow-and-white fruiting tomatoes, which seem suspended in midair at night.

Include fragrant herbs in the garden scheme—they not only look pretty during the day and are edible,

The striking flower of Epiphyllum crenatum, left, appears only at night. Right: Bright yellow flowers such as sundrops glow in the waning sunlight.

but they smell nice when the foliage is gently brushed. Golden sage and tricolor sage, with their lighter colors, show up well in the evening, as do many of the variegated thymes.

It is not difficult to create a well-balanced evening garden. There are essentially 11 elements on the palette from which the evening gardener may paint. For a balanced and successful garden, choose one or more plants from each of the 11 categories.

Sculpture & Silhouette includes plants grown for their architectural interest, especially when illuminated or contrasted against a white wall or the evening sky.

Textured Bark comprises trees and shrubs that have bark that is interesting at night, whether white, like some birches, or with an unusual pattern that shows up when subtly lighted.

Flowers Aglow at Sunset includes those with darker blue, purple and cerise flowers that come alive in the late afternoon light.

Bright Flowers are the orange and yellow flowers that show up so brilliantly as the light continues to dim and that bridge the gap between day and evening.

Pale Flowers on the Ground includes low-growing plants that have light-colored blooms which show up in early evening.

White Flowers comprises the many plants that have white flowers, which are easily visible in an evening garden.

Night Bloomers are those special additions that flower only at night.

The **Silver Foliage** plants reflect moonlight and are almost as visible

as white flowers.

Foliage for Contrast includes plants that have the benefit of lighter-colored variegations that come alive against the darker portions of foliage.

Fragrant Plants includes flowers that are only aromatic at night, as well as those that are fragrant around the clock.

The final grouping is the **Stars of the Evening Garden**—a collection of my favorites, chosen from each of the other groups.

The species discussed in this book are my personal choices. There are many other plants that can work—think of your own favorites as you read through the plant selections. As long as the plant can be seen in the light of an evening garden, by all means include it. Each garden is, after all, a reflection of its creator and owner.

Once you've made your plant selections, the pleasure begins: laying out the garden—first on paper and then getting down and dirty in the soil. Have fun. It will be a garden you will enjoy for many years—both day and night.

Sculpture & Silhouette

Dried flower stalks add to the interest of ornamental grasses in autumn and winter.

WHEN YOU CONSIDER the subtleties of an evening garden, it is important to include at least one plant for its dramatic effect and strong architectural statement. If an evening garden is to be of interest year-round, architectural plants will carry the garden through the barren winter months. Even the branching habits of common trees, such as oaks and maples, are noticeable without the diversion of leaves, especially when illuminated at night.

Plants of architectural interest act like living sculptures in a garden and can be an extension of the garden's man-made architectural features. A large palm tree, if accented with lighting from above or below, can easily be a focal point of the garden, and a saguaro cactus with the full moon behind it is truly a work of art.

The form of architectural plants makes them a welcome addition to the evening garden, especially when used in combination with lighting. Even a northern gardener can grow a

small palm tree or cactus in a container indoors in winter and carry it outdoors in summer.

Once the plant is outside, its placement will determine its effect in the garden. Place it by itself, in the middle of a lawn, and accent it with small spotlights at its base. Set it in front of a white wall and light it from below—vivid shadows will be cast on the wall. Another alternative is to place the plant behind a piece of material or a Japanese shoji screen. Aim lights from behind the plant toward the screen. This will cast a subtle or bold silhouette on the screen, depending on the intensity of the light and the distance between the plant and the screen.

Evergreens come in all shapes, sizes and colors and are great focal points in the evening garden in both winter and summer. New dwarf varieties are introduced each year—some have needles with bluish or golden tones that are noticeable in the evening. Other broad-leaved evergreen trees and shrubs, such as hollies, should also be considered for the evening garden.

Large ornamental grasses and bamboos make a good background upon which the evening garden is built. Some varieties are variegated, which makes them more noticeable at night. All large grasses and bamboos have the additional benefit of adding sound to the garden. The soft sighing made by a breeze blowing through a stand of grass is very relaxing, as is the soughing of a large pine tree as the wind rustles through its branches.

Some plants, like yucca, have very straight, strong lines, while others, like the corkscrew willow, have gnarled, contorted branches. When planning your garden, consider contrasting plants with vertical lines with those that have twisting branches or have a more prostrate form.

Contrary to popular belief, some bamboo species are hardy even in northern growing areas, where they provide sensory delight day and night.

Bamboos

ALTHOUGH MANY people think bamboo is a tropical plant, there are many varieties that will grow in cold climates. It is true that bamboos are native to tropical forests in a broad equatorial belt from 40 degrees S to 40 degrees N, but within that range they grow in altitudes up to 9,800 feet and can therefore withstand extremes of temperature.

A friend of mine on Long Island has a large bamboo grove that provides a lovely backdrop and a privacy screen for his garden. One of the best bamboo collections in the eastern United States is near Boston, not exactly an area known for its balmy winters.

Most gardeners know very little about bamboos, despite the huge number of listed species. (There are about 1,200 species at present.) There is a great deal of misinformation in circulation, most of which is unfortunately accepted as fact. Bamboos grow in almost any climate except the frozen polar regions. On the West Coast and in the South, the number of cultivated varieties that can be grown is almost limitless. Northern gardeners also have many hardy varieties from which to choose.

As an evergreen, bamboo makes a good background for other lighter-colored plants in the evening garden. Look to varieties with variegated foliage or interesting stalks, such as the golden bamboo with golden-yellow stems and green stripes—they add another dimension of interest to the evening garden. To best appreciate bamboos, it is wise to follow the Asiatic tradition of thinning them so that individual stems are distinguishable.

Bamboos can be separated into two general categories: running and clumping types. Running varieties require some means of keeping their roots or rhizomes from wandering into unwanted areas. But that is not an entirely unpleasant chore. Many years ago, I moved into a house with bamboo in the garden. In the spring, when I discovered new shoots poking up through the gravel driveway, I simply cut them off, sliced them into bite-sized pieces, boiled them and threw them into a stir-fry of chicken and vegetables.

Culinary considerations aside, containment is best accomplished with a concrete barrier extending two feet below ground, although other materials may be used. A friend who has a lovely bamboo collection keeps his groves and specimen plants within bounds simply by mowing the turf that surrounds the beds.

If the idea of planting a running variety strikes fear into your heart, there are safe alternatives: clumping bamboos. Plant them with the assurance that they will remain well-

A clump of feathery bamboo is handsome when seen from above.

behaved, mannerly and controlled, and will never covet their neighbor's space. A friend's patch of umbrella bamboo has been growing happily in her garden for about eight years without intruding on the space in front of it reserved for annuals or stretching out to the side and invading the neighboring rhododendron.

The attractiveness of bamboo is well established in garden design. Bamboo is traditional in Chinese and Japanese gardens, symbolizing suppleness and power, true friendship and vigorous age. Observe an established grove or a mature potted bamboo and you are in for a sensory delight. Breezes gently playing through the graceful foliage can conjure up momentary vacations or flights of fancy. Sounds created by the movement of air can mimic the soothing murmur of the sea.

Illuminate the bamboo at night by spotlighting it either from above to accentuate the foliage and create interesting shadows, or from below to focus attention on the stems of the plants. If lighting is used well, with an eye toward texture and form, it will accentuate the beauty and grace of these magnificent and versatile plants.

You can grow all of the recommended bamboos in containers. Place the container on a rolling stand so you can move the plant around to fill in a dull area. When a small shrub or perennial has finished blooming and is in a prime area of your patio, simply roll in the bamboo and illuminate it for a quick change of pace.

Bamboos are members of the grass family and have many similarities to both their domesticated and wild cousins. This relationship is an important consideration in the care of these plants.

Bamboos thrive in fertile, well-drained soil with ample organic content and a neutral pH. Add an organic mulch or compost twice a year. Most appreciate full sun, with the exception of the clumping varieties, which need some protection from direct sun. Maintain evenly moist soil, especially until the plants become established. In cool areas, mulch heavily each fall to protect the rhizomes during the winter months. If treated to the same organic cultural practices as your lawn, bamboos will perform admirably and flourish.

NONINVASIVE CLUMPING BAMBOOS

UMBRELLA BAMBOO— FARGESIA MURIELAE (SINARUNDINARIA MURIELAE)

UMBRELLA BAMBOO has a beauty and grace that enhances any evening garden. The long, narrow leaves are bright green and rustle gently in a breeze. The ½-inch-diameter green culms, or stalks, grow to 12 feet tall, arching gracefully. This is an exceptionally beautiful noninvasive plant.

Plant umbrella bamboo alone in a large clump and subtly illuminate it to best show it off. Or place it at the back of the garden, where its form can be appreciated silhouetted against the night sky.

Umbrella bamboo is native to the cold mountains of China in areas inhabited by pandas, which relish it as a food source. It can grow well in most of North America as it is hardy to −15 degrees F. This bamboo will grow in sun or semishade.

The shiny stems of black bamboo are prized in the evening garden.

FOUNTAIN BAMBOO— FARGESIA NITIDA (SINARUNDINARIA NITIDA)

THE FIRST TIME I came across fountain bamboo in an evening garden, I did not know what it was. A multitude of narrow leaves shimmered in the moonlight at eye level and reached high above my head.

Indeed it is well-named, as *nitida* means "shining" in Latin. The bright green leaves catch the moonlight in such a way that they glimmer majestically. The ½-inch-diameter culms grow slowly to a height of 12 feet.

Another point of interest for the evening gardener is that the culms are covered with a bluish-white powder when immature that shows up nicely when lighted from below or in the light of a full moon. At maturity, the culms become an attractive dark purple.

A friend who had fountain bam-

boo in her garden used to illuminate it so it could be shown off at any time, regardless of the cycle of the moon. After a year, she removed the lights. She felt that seeing this bamboo every night in its shimmering glory was like eating lobster or some other delicacy every night for dinner.

This bamboo grows best in partial shade, especially in areas with hot, dry summers. Reliable to −20 degrees F, it is considered to be the most hardy bamboo in America.

RUNNING BAMBOOS

BLACK BAMBOO— PHYLLOSTACHYS NIGRA

IRONICALLY, IT IS the shiny black stems of this bamboo that are prized in the evening garden. It is absolutely stunning when spotlights shine up at the stems from ground level, as you don't expect to see black at night in a garden.

The culms of this eye-catcher start

out green and turn black within six months to a year. It grows to about 30 feet, with culms that are 3 inches in diameter. If this running variety is given a large enough plot, it will establish an impressive grove. Lighting plants with such large culms provides a dramatic focal point.

Black bamboo flourishes in full sun and is hardy to 0 degrees F.

HENON BAMBOO—
PHYLLOSTACHYS NIGRA
'HENON'

THIS IS ANOTHER bamboo that will grow to a substantial size and can be very impressive in an evening garden, provided you have the space and height required to show it off. The culms have been reported to grow to 55 feet high and attain a diameter of 3½ inches. This selected cultivar has green culms that show off majestically when illuminated from above or below.

Five-foot-tall Sasa veitchii bamboo is perfect for the small garden.

One of the most striking uses of henon bamboo I have seen was in a Japanese garden planted by a pond. The lighting was very subtle, coming from soft floodlights hanging in nearby trees aimed at the bamboo. Walking from a relatively wooded area along a narrow path, rounding a bend and coming upon the sight of the massive bamboo coupled with its reflection in the still pond was breathtaking.

As a running bamboo, henon will spread to whatever boundary you establish. It grows well in full sun and is hardy to 0 degrees F.

PLEIOBLASTUS
VIRIDISTRIATUS
(ARUNDINARIA AURICOMA)

THIS BAMBOO, with its striking golden-yellow leaves with brilliant green stripes, provides an accent in the evening garden even without artificial illumination, but when illuminated from above, it glows.

Pleioblastus only grows to about 2 feet high with ¼-inch-diameter culms. Its diminutive size makes it perfect as an accent plant in a garden of any size. I saw it used in a California garden to soften the line from a stone wall to a gravel path—it made a lovely tall ground cover, especially vibrant in the moonlight. In a container, I have seen it brighten up the corner of a small terrace.

Grow this bamboo in full sun to partial shade. Provide a barrier to keep it from creeping into other areas, although it does not tend to be

very aggressive. It is hardy to 0 degrees F.

KUMAZASA—SASA VEITCHII

IF YOU ARE INTIMIDATED by the large varieties of bamboo and do not want one as small as *Pleioblastus viridistriatus*, this is the bamboo for you. It is perfect for a small garden: It grows only 5 feet tall and has ¼-inch-diameter culms. Include it in the evening garden for its winter interest, when the dark green leaves dry and develop wide buff-colored margins. This gives the illusion of variegation, making kumazasa very visible in the evening garden.

I saw it growing at Longwood Gardens in planting beds in the parking lot. With the cream-colored edges of the leaves very visible, there is no danger of anyone driving into the beds at night.

Kumazasa grows best in partial shade and is hardy to −15 degrees F.

Cacti & Succulents

DON'T JUST SKIP over this section simply because you live outside the Southwest. Although most people associate cacti with desert areas and warm climates, there is a cactus native to Long Island where I live— one of the prickly pear cacti, *Opuntia humifusa*.

In areas where the winters are too cold, cacti can be grown in containers and brought into a well-lighted room or greenhouse for the winter.

Although most people associate cactus with the desert, cold-climate gardeners can grow them in containers that are brought inside.

In the evening garden, their shape is captivating when illuminated by moonlight, lighted from behind or silhouetted against a white wall.

Cacti range in height from several inches to over 50 feet. The large species can be grown effectively in semitropical regions in low-water landscapes.

Cacti in the landscape need full sun and well-drained soil. Water newly planted cacti sparingly to avoid rotting the dormant roots. Once the new roots are active, within four to six weeks, water thoroughly then allow the soil to dry be-

fore watering again. In the fall, cut back on watering to allow the plants to go dormant. Feed monthly in the spring and summer.

GOLDEN BARREL CACTUS— ECHINOCACTUS GRUSONII

INCLUDE THE GOLDEN barrel cactus in the evening garden for its unique form and color—it has a wonderful rounded shape.

The golden barrel is slow-growing, never getting larger than 3 or 4 feet tall and 2½ feet in diameter. Often baby plants grow right alongside

the original plant, giving the effect of an undulating cluster in the moonlight.

Although the pronounced ribs of the cactus itself are green, the stout, showy thorns that cover the cactus are sunny yellow, making it outstanding in dim light. It blooms in April or May—1½- to 2-inch-wide yellow flowers sprout on the top of the plant.

Water once every two weeks in the summer. In desert areas, provide some shade. In cool areas, protect it from frost and grow under lights indoors in winter.

PRICKLY PEAR CACTI—
OPUNTIA SP.

When I lived in Portugal, I became well acquainted with the large prickly pear cacti that grow 5 or 6 feet tall. Their branching stems that are jointed in large, rounded, flattened pads seemed to reach up into the night sky when I viewed them during midnight strolls.

Flowers appear at the top of the pads in midsummer, followed by the fruit—the prickly pear. Prickly pear flowers are red or yellow and measure up to 3 inches in diameter.

Prickly pears need little or no water once they are established. Plant them in well-drained soil in full sun. Depending on the variety, prickly pear cacti may be hardy to Zone 6.

Evergreens

Almost any evergreen can be considered for inclusion in an evening garden. From the tallest dawn redwood to the blue carpet of 'Bar Harbor' juniper, each has its own particular quality to recommend it.

Conifers and other needled trees are included with evergreens, yet some of the needled trees, like the larch, are deciduous and lose their leaves in autumn. Evergreens also encompass a large group of broad-leaved plants like hollies, osmanthus, rhododendrons and pineapple guava.

There are far too many evergreens to even begin to describe in detail. Yet, when broken down into evening possibilities, the numbers become more manageable and the choices easier to make.

Suffice to say that, with their various forms, colors, shapes and sizes, they provide a good anchor for the evening garden. This is especially true in winter in cold climates when the landscape is essentially colorless. Nothing is quite so beautiful as snow-covered evergreens glimmering in the moonlight.

DWARF EVERGREENS

Dwarf evergreens are genetically smaller and often slower growing than the same variety in a normal size.

Even when the name "dwarf" is attached, find out what the ultimate size of a plant will be before you buy it. Although a shrub may be cute only 2 feet tall when you bring it home from the nursery, it may grow to 10 feet and may not be what you had in mind.

Some dwarf plants can be encouraged to keep within bounds by judicious pruning and limiting their growing space by keeping them in a container. Dwarf citrus trees (hardy

only in Zones 9 and 10) are perfect container plants that can be moved indoors in cooler areas.

The Meserve hollies (*Ilex meserveae*), including the blue series ('Blue Boy,' 'Blue Girl'), are dependably hardy on Long Island, where

they were developed. They usually grow no more than 5 feet tall.

Also consider the numerous forms of junipers (hardy from Zone 10), including ones with creeping or prostrate forms, like *Juniperus horizontalis.* 'Glauca' has attractive steel-blue sprays of slender needles that are gorgeous in the moonlight.

Try one of the dwarf varieties of pine. I have a dwarf red pine that has stayed at a height of 15 inches for six years—perfect for the night-time poolside garden covered with a

Some prickly pear cacti, opposite, *can be grown as far north as Long Island.* **Below:** *With a wide variety of interesting shapes and forms, evergreens provide a good anchor for the evening garden.*

Eucalyptus is majestic in the setting sun. In spring, its white flowers are a bonus.

is in shadow—an exquisite sight.

If you are lucky to live in an area where you can grow southern magnolia (hardy in Zones 7–10), try planting *Magnolia grandiflora*. It is a majestic beauty: its shiny, broad leaves reflect moonlight, and its large, fragrant white flowers grow up to 12 inches in diameter and last through the summer and fall—a bonus for the evening garden.

EVERGREENS WITH FLOWERS

In addition to those already mentioned, some evergreens have interesting flowers that make them a pleasant addition to an evening garden.

The strawberry tree (*Arbutus unedo*) has edible fruit and small white to pinkish urn-shaped flowers that appear in fall and winter, interspersed among some of the previous year's ¾-inch yellow to red fruits. This tree is hardy from Zone 7 to 9.

The pineapple guava (*Feijoa sellowiana*) has oval, glossy green leaves with silvery undersides. A new variety is available with variegated leaves. The spectacular 1-inch edible flowers resemble succulent fuchsia blossoms—pearly white outside and purplish inside. In autumn, the luscious grayish-green fruits ripen.

I first saw the pineapple guava in California. When I saw the handsome leaves and tasted the edible flowers, I was immediately smitten. I ordered one from Wayside Gardens and planted it in a sheltered location against my house. Before the first frost, I pot it up and bring it inside,

light gravel mulch that shows this pine off to perfection.

EVERGREENS FOR IMPACT

Other evergreens may be included in the evening garden for their dramatic impact. Cedars (hardy in Zones 6–9) are fast-growing with conical or pyramidal shapes. Carob, or St. John's bread (*Ceratonia siliqua*), which is hardy in only the warmest parts of the country (Zones 9–10), has a pleasing rounded shape and grows to about 20 feet.

Eucalyptus (hardy in Zones 7–10, depending on the variety) is a fast-growing tree, usually with attractive, light-colored peeling bark. The leaves may be fragrant, and the white flowers are a nice bonus in spring. My aunt has a eucalyptus in her California garden that rises high above the house and the rest of the hillside garden. It is strategically placed to catch the last rays of the afternoon sun even when the rest of the garden

Evening Gardens

where I enjoy the foliage all winter. When the weather warms, out it goes again, potted into a larger container. Even though it is only hardy from Zone 8 to 10, I can grow it in Zone 6 as long as I keep it from frost in winter.

Sweetshade (*Hymenosporum flavum*) is another broad-leaved evergreen hardy in Zones 9 and 10. Its large, oblong, shiny dark green leaves are handsome when softly illuminated from above. The added bonus is the golden-yellow flowers that smell like orange blossoms from April to September.

VARIEGATED EVERGREENS

EVERGREENS NEED not necessarily be green. There are beautiful variegated hollies whose leaves are outstanding in an evening garden with their cream-colored edges.

'Crippsii,' one variety of hinoki false cypress (*Chamaecyparis obtusa*), has yellow-colored foliage that is lovely in the late afternoon and early evening.

I first saw 'Silverdust' leyland cypress (x *Cupressocyparis leylandii* 'Silverdust') nestled among other leyland cypresses at the end of a long day of garden touring in England. With its creamy-white variegated foliage, it seemed to shine like a beacon in the last rays of sun.

The blue spruce (*Picea pungens glauca*) has a coating on its green needles that makes them appear blue. In almost any light, it looks as if it is being viewed in full moonlight.

Ferns

FERNS ARE INTERESTING in the evening garden because of the shape of their leaves, or fronds. They are best showcased by subtly lighting them either from above or, if they are low-growing and border a path, with path lights that illuminate a circle around their bases. Ferns that have an upright form make a good foil against a low white wall. Ferns range in height from several inches to more than 30 feet (tree ferns). Although most people think of ferns as woodland plants, there are varieties that grow in deserts, open fields and mountainous areas.

MAIDENHAIR FERN (FIVE-FINGER FERN)— ADIANTUM PEDATUM

THIS NATIVE North American fern has fronds that fork and form fingerlike patterns on slender 1- to 2½-foot-long stems.

I first saw maidenhair as a possibility for the evening garden when I was photographing a friend's yard late in the day. Before I knew it, the light had faded and I had yet to see the woodland garden. As I walked into the area, I was surprised to see how visible some of the ferns' delicate forms were in the moonlight. The fern was growing next to a very light variegated hosta. Some of the fronds overlapped the hosta leaves, creating interesting patterns of light and dark. Its delicate appearance was enhanced by moonlight.

Grow maidenhair fern as a container plant in rich, well-drained soil. It will be happy indoors in winter and outside in summer. However, since it is hardy in most areas of the country (Zones 3–8), you can also plant it outdoors in a shady spot in rich, moist humus. A pine needle mulch around the fern creates the illusion of a woodland garden while conserving moisture near the roots.

CINNAMON FERN— OSMUNDA CINNAMOMEA

ALTHOUGH THIS FERN is handsome anytime during the growing season, it should be placed where it will be a focal point of the midspring garden. At that time, the silvery crosiers, or fiddleheads, emerge from the still-damp earth.

When I first saw the new growth one evening, it looked like clumps of

The silvery fiddleheads of cinnamon fern look like narrow question marks.

narrow question marks punctuating the woodland. Cinnamon ferns are so different from anything else I have in the garden; I eagerly await their emergence each spring.

This relatively tall 2- to 4-foot-high fern develops two types of fronds. The sterile fronds are broad, pinnate and blue-green. The fertile fronds give rise to its name. They have spikes of spores that, when ripe in late spring or early summer, turn a rich cinnamon color. Cinnamon ferns require lots of water and grow best in rich loam with good drainage. They are hardy to Zone 4.

ROYAL FERN— OSMUNDA REGALIS

THE ROYAL FERN is one of the stateliest of the hardy ferns. A 5-foot fern silhouetted in front of a white wall makes a striking focal point in any evening garden.

Christmas ferns stay green year-round, even in cold regions.

This plant has a fairly upright habit. Rather broad leaflets make up each frond. In early spring, the young fronds are a reddish-pink that is accented by the setting sun.

Like its relative the cinnamon fern, the royal fern grows best in rich, fertile, loamy well-drained soil. Hardy to Zone 3, it can be grown into the far northern reaches of the United States and southern Canada.

CHRISTMAS FERN— POLYSTICHUM ACROSTICHOIDES

ADD A CHRISTMAS fern to your evening garden for the beautiful form of a fern year-round—it is evergreen. It is also one of the most commonly grown ferns native to eastern North America.

I have seen it planted next to the silvery leaves of dusty miller. The plants contrast handsomely with each other, providing continual garden interest. The narrow, pinnate fronds are shiny green and somewhat leathery, growing 1 to 2 feet long.

Grow the Christmas fern outdoors in rich, moist humus. Mulch around the plant to keep the roots from drying out. It is hardy to Zone 4.

Ornamental Perennial Grasses

I HAVE BEEN A lover and grower of ornamental grasses for some time—even before they came into fashion. I first realized how useful they are in the evening garden when I chanced to go for a midnight swim at a friend's. Foolishly, I removed my glasses before I dove into the pool. To my nearsighted eyes, the only indication of the end of the pool was what appeared to be a pale blue, almost luminous swath of vegetation. As I got close, I realized that it was a large planting of blue fescue, one of the more diminutive grasses.

The larger grasses, which can range up to 10 feet tall, are equally striking in an evening garden. For drama, try spotlighting them from either above or below. Variegated grasses have the added evening interest of lighter striations.

With hundreds of species and varieties, and a diversity of sizes and colors, there are ornamental grasses for every garden. They are commonly grown for contrast in mixed borders, as ground covers and edging, for privacy and screening, and as specimen plants to provide a vertical accent.

The feathery flower stalks in summer add to their interest. Tall grasses make a wonderful rustling sound as twilight breezes blow through them—all part of the illusion created by an evening garden.

Before the autumn frost, I cut several flowering branches and some long leaves from a large clump of grasses and stick them into the soil in a whiskey barrel on my front patio. It livens up the look of the otherwise dreary patio at night and provides a waiting area for birds attracted to the nearby bird feeder.

I especially enjoy the tall grasses during the fall and winter. In autumn, pigment recedes from the leaves, leaving the grasses buff- or

Tall ornamental grasses make a wonderful rustling sound as the twilight breezes blow through them.

wheat-colored for the winter. Their light color and strong form are great in the fall and winter evening garden contrasted with the wonderful shapes of the evergreens. They also provide shelter and food for birds and wildlife during the cold months.

Ornamental perennial grasses are easy to grow. The challenge is not how to grow them, but how to keep them from spreading and encroaching on the rest of the garden.

Many of the grasses spread by runners. Restrict their growth by inserting a sheet of metal 12 inches deep to define the area where you want them to grow. Another option is to grow them in sunken containers with ample drainage holes. Once they are established in the garden, the large varieties, like miscanthus, are nearly impossible to dig out unless you have access to a backhoe. Make sure you plant the right variety in the right spot. Allow for a clump to at least double in size.

In general, ornamental perennial grasses need little care and retain their looks for most of the year. They will thrive in most soil types, as long as the soil is well drained. Grow grasses in full sun. In spring, they must be cut back to the ground, so for about six weeks, they are not very attractive. The new shoots grow quickly, however, and are soon lush and full, gently swaying in the breeze.

PAMPAS GRASS (CORTADERIA SELLOANA)

IF YOU HAVE ever seen the plumes of pampas grass in the light of a harvest moon—dramatic and white-flowering—you know why it is an impressive plant in an evening garden.

Pampas grass is one of the best known ornamental grasses. A single clump of grayish blue-green cascading leaves grows up to 5 feet tall and nearly as wide. The impressive flower stalk rises almost twice as high as the autumn foliage.

The best pampas grass planting I have seen was on the corner of a piece of property in southern California. The flowering plumes of the pampas grass were highly visible from all directions and screened the house from the road. For the most dramatic effect in an evening garden, light the grass with floodlights from the base.

Ornamental grasses need little care and retain their looks for most of the year.

Pampas grass needs moist soil and good drainage, especially in the winter. Unfortunately, it is hardy in only the warmer areas of the country (to Zone 8). It can be grown in a barrel and brought inside for the winter to prevent it from freezing, but that may require too much effort and take up more space than most gardeners have.

BLUE FESCUE—FESTUCA OVINA GLAUCA

A SINGLE PLANT or a large planting of these charming, blue-tinged grasses can be effective in an evening garden. At night, the color of the plant is soft, yet glowing. The 8-inch-long slender blades form a pale blue-green hummock.

Blue fescue will liven up any border, acting as an accent plant near the front, or it can be used in a group planting. As a large planting, it makes an unusual ground cover. The pale color of this grass makes it visible without artificial lighting, but it is enhanced by soft spotlights aimed down on it from above.

Blue fescue grows best in rich, well-drained soil in full sun. It is hardy to Zone 4.

MAIDEN GRASS—MISCANTHUS SINENSIS 'GRACILLIMUS'

MAIDEN GRASS IS a favorite that I included in the garden by my landlady's pool. In the

evening, the white midvein on the ¼-inch blades is subtly visible. The foliage is long and fine, growing up to 7 feet long. The clump is narrow and erect at the base, yet curves gently near the top of the blades. Its graceful arching form is lovely silhouetted against the evening sky or a light background. To add to its beauty, white fan-shaped flowers rise above the foliage in autumn.

I have interplanted other interesting miscanthus cultivars by the swimming pool to act as a privacy screen. During the day, you are drawn to the overall effect of the grass planting; at night, the differences in the variegations are highlighted by two post lamps on either side.

Variegated miscanthus (*M. sinensis* 'Variegatus') has distinct green and white vertical stripes. Porcupine grass (*M. sinensis strictus*) makes a somewhat bold statement with bright green 6-foot-long blades with yellow horizontal bands. It has an almost rigid upright habit that is not easily beaten down by heavy rains.

Miscanthus grows best in full sun and well-drained soil. When planting, allow at least 5 feet between plants. Miscanthus is reliably hardy in Zones 5 and 6, and can be grown in a sheltered south-facing location in Zone 4.

Palm Trees

THE GRACEFUL FORM and exotic beauty of a palm tree is even more pro-

Only 6 feet tall, the pygmy date palm can be grown even by novice gardeners.

nounced after sundown. Whether silhouetted against the sky or a light-colored background, lighted from above or below or not illuminated at all, a palm stands out in any garden.

Northern gardeners should note that there are palms hardy enough to grow outside year-round in Portland (Oregon) and Seattle. If you live in a warmer area, you can choose from a wide selection of palms to accent your landscape. Even if you live in a very cold area, you can grow one of the dwarf varieties indoors during the winter and move it outdoors in summer. Consider getting a planter with casters to make it easier to move even a dwarf palm in and out of the house with the seasons.

PYGMY DATE PALM— PHOENIX ROEBELENII

THIS IS A SMALL palm that anyone can grow—it reaches only 6 feet in height. In most areas, it can be grown as a houseplant. Don't be afraid to bring your houseplants outdoors in the summer to use them as accent plants.

The pygmy date palm's feathery leaves form a dense crown on its short stem. One of the most dramatic uses of a palm I have seen was achieved by placing this palm behind a Japanese shoji screen. A floodlight was placed behind the plant. The silhouette was striking, viewed from the other side of the screen.

Desert fan palms tower to 40 feet.

This palm needs a lot of light. Inside, place it under a grow light; outdoors, plant it in partial shade. For best results, keep the soil just moist. It is hardy in the Southwest.

WINDMILL PALM (CHUSAN PALM)— CHAMAEROPS EXCELSA

THE WINDMILL PALM has a marvelous shape for an evening garden with broad fan-shaped leaves that are striking in silhouette. The leaves grow up to 2½ feet long and 4 feet wide and do resemble the blades of a windmill. It has an unbranched trunk covered with coarse brown fibers—an un-usual feature which is striking at night when lit from the base.

The windmill palm is very slow growing, but it can eventually reach a height of 20 feet. In cold climates, it can be grown in a large container, so long as it gets sufficient light indoors in the winter. Outside, the palm needs full sun. It will grow in relatively poor soil and responds well to water and plant food.

The windmill palm does not transplant well. It is the hardiest palm, however, growing happily any place where frost is not prolonged and winter temperatures do not drop below 10 degrees F.

DESERT FAN PALM— WASHINGTONIA FILIFERA

WHEN I FIRST visited southern California, I was in awe of the tall silhouettes of the desert fan palms against the western sky at sunset. Just when I thought the show was over, the moon rose and the silhouettes were still breathtaking. That sight is firmly etched in my brain, and I call it up whenever I'm shivering in the snow and sleet of winter at home.

The desert fan palm is one of the many large palm trees that provide architectural interest in a tropical or subtropical evening garden. With its erect cylindrical stem, it can grow 40 feet or higher. The stem's upper portion is partially covered with with-ered leaves that, when they finally fall off, leave a scar on the bark, giving the appearance of striped rings.

I have seen a young palm illumi-nated from ground level with lights aimed up the trunk to the leaves—it was very impressive.

This palm will tolerate desert heat and some drought, but it thrives on moisture in well-drained soil. Young trees can be grown in containers in cool areas and moved inside for the winter.

Other Plants of Architectural Interest

WHILE MOST bamboos, evergreens, cacti, ferns and palms can be used in the evening garden, there are many plants that don't fit into a particular category, but which still provide shape and form in the evening garden. Whether graceful or stark, twisted or straight, the lines of these plants serve as a focal point, especially when illuminated.

SAGO PALM (CYCAD)— CYCAS REVOLUTA

THE SAGO PALM is worth considering in the evening garden because, during its lifetime, it goes through two distinct forms, both of which are of architectural interest.

This palm looks like a fern when it is young (less than 3 feet tall) and then grows slowly to a height of 10 feet. At this point, it looks like a palm. However, it is neither; it is a primitive plant called a cycad, which is related to modern-day conifers.

The 2- to 3-foot-long featherlike

leaves grow out in rosettes from a central point on top of a single trunk. They are divided into many narrow, glossy, dark green leathery segments.

Although not hardy in cold areas, the sago palm is dramatic as a potted plant in the northern garden in summer. For a unique effect, try softly lighting it from either side.

Cycads are great container plants and may be trained as bonsai. They prefer partial shade and moist, rich, well-drained soil. They are hardy in southern and desert areas.

PALMELLA (SOAP TREE, NARROW-LEAF YUCCA)— YUCCA ELATA

I ENVY GARDENERS in the Southwest who can grow this yucca outside year-round. At night, illuminate the stems from below or light it from above to cast bizarre shadows on the ground.

The word *palmella* is Spanish for small palm, and the plant does resemble a small palm tree. Long clusters of 2-inch waxy white flowers appear in spring at the ends of the stalks and soften the look of the plant. Its stark form, with a prominent stem covered in dried straw-colored leaves, bears two or more crowns of spine-tipped bright green leaves.

Yucca elata is native to the grasslands and deserts from western Texas to central and southern Ari-

The most common yucca in eastern landscapes, Adam's needle produces creamy-white flowers in the summer.

zona at elevations ranging from 1,500 to 6,000 feet.

Yuccas are most commonly purchased in nurseries or garden centers, but with patience, a yucca can be grown from seed. A small plant may take five years or more before it begins to bloom. Grow in well-drained, sandy loam in full sun. Hardy to Zone 8, it is difficult to grow outside of its native Southwest.

ADAM'S NEEDLE— YUCCA FILAMENTOSA

A LTHOUGH I CANNOT grow the palmella in my Long Island garden, I can grow this yucca, also known as Adam's needle. Its effect in the evening garden is different from its southwestern cousin as this hardy 3-foot-tall yucca is almost stemless, with just a clump of the stiff, pointed leaves. This plant is distinguished by long, curly white threads on the leaf margins.

I saw an Adam's needle in a Connecticut garden planted near a white wall. During the day it was attractive, but at night it was the star of the garden. The lighting was placed in front and slightly off to the side of the yucca, so that the light shone through the plant and cast an over-

Fennel can make an attractive and fragrant landscape plant.

sized shadow on the wall.

This is the most commonly grown yucca in eastern landscapes. In summer, it sprouts a flower spike up to 6 feet tall with large creamy-white bell-shaped flowers.

Like its southwestern cousin, it is slow to grow and prefers well-drained sandy loam and full sun. It is hardy to Zone 5.

VARIEGATED GRASSY-LEAVED SWEET FLAG—ACORUS GRAMINEUS 'VARIEGATUS'

Two of the key characteristics for a plant in an evening garden come together in this plant: a strong form and variegated foliage that stands out in dim light. It is one of the few plants grown for architectural interest that can be put near the front of the evening garden and will be noticed without artificial lighting.

This hardy perennial is in the arum family and is grown for its fans of grasslike leaves that resemble tufts of iris. The white-edged leaves grow to 1½ feet tall.

This plant is very versatile. You can grow it in a bog garden or at the edge of a pond. It will also do well in a low-water landscape and hold its own among grasses, bamboos and other sword-leaved plants. It is hardy in all zones.

FENNEL—FOENICULUM VULGARE

I had never seen fennel used as a landscape plant nor considered it an evening plant until I visited California and Vancouver Island, British Columbia.

In several gardens and at Fetzer Vineyards, I saw bronze fennel in the late afternoon. The warm color of the feathery 3- to 4-foot foliage glowed in the rays of the setting sun. Later, it was illuminated, giving a soft, sensuous effect as it was caught in a breeze.

At Sooke Harbour House in British Columbia, the more common fennel grew wild on the hillsides. It was beautiful in late summer, with the full moon illuminating its graceful green foliage and flat clusters of tiny yellow flowers.

Fennel is a perennial herb that is often grown as an annual. Its stems are blue-green, glossy and somewhat flattened at the base. The foliage is bright green and feathery.

The flowers do not appear until the summer of the second year. By fall, the flowers have matured, producing ¼-inch gray-green seeds.

The plant itself gives off a strong anise scent, so be sure to place it in the garden where you can lightly brush against it.

Fennel grows happily in average garden soil. In mild areas, sow fennel seeds in early spring. In colder areas, seed fennel into the garden in July.

The twisted shape of the Japanese maple is attractive in the moonlight, particularly on snowy winter evenings.

Of course, like many of the other herbs, small fennel plants are available at nurseries and garden centers. This annual can be planted anytime in spring, after the danger of frost has passed. Allow at least 8 inches between plants.

CUT-LEAF JAPANESE MAPLE—
ACER PALMATUM 'DISSECTUM'

THIS MAPLE FIRST caught my eye one snowy evening many years ago. The twisted shape and subtle musculature of its branches

was highlighted by the moonlight and snow.

One is now planted near my front door, where I can enjoy it by moonlight in winter or softly illuminated with a spotlight in summer. Of all the Japanese maples, the cut-leaf has perhaps the best architectural form, coupled with a lovely leaf shape and color. The plant itself arches to form a somewhat dome-shaped, symmetrical shrub. Even at maturity, the tree is no more than 6 feet tall, with a somewhat wider spread.

The leaves are reminiscent of lace. In spring, the young leaves are light green. They turn reddish-green by summer and finally go out in a burst

The corkscrew willow, **opposite,** *is best appreciated when leafless.*
Below: *Harry Lauder's walking stick.*

of brilliant orange flame in autumn that is especially beautiful at sunset. There are purple-leaved forms that also have good autumn foliage.

Japanese maples grow best in light-dappled shade, as strong summer sun can scorch the leaves. They prefer rich, humusy soil that is slightly acidic, but they will grow in slightly alkaline soil if they are kept moist enough. Pruning is not necessary, but some gardeners prefer to prune the lower branches to lift the tree. These maples are hardy to Zone 5.

ROCKSPRAY COTONEASTER
(HERRINGBONE
COTONEASTER)—
COTONEASTER
HORIZONTALIS

THIS COTONEASTER is perfect trained against a low white wall or trellis, where its herringbone pattern can be appreciated in an evening garden. Only 2 feet tall, it is handsome with gray-green horizontal branches that spread out into the shape of a fan, while maintaining their unique herringbone design.

Evening Gardens

In late summer, this shrub produces berries that attract birds to the garden. The small gray to gray-green leaves turn bright red in fall.

Consider cotoneaster for the evening garden, especially in winter, as it is semievergreen and only loses its leaves when planted at the northern edge of its hardiness range (Zone 5). Grow in full sun and well-drained soil.

HARRY LAUDER'S WALKING STICK—CORYLUS AVELLANA 'CONTORTA'

NAMED FOR A British vaudevillian who popularized it by using a branch as a cane in his song-and-dance routines, this wonderfully contorted shrub is most interesting in the evening garden in fall and winter, after it has lost its leaves.

Peering at the grotesquely shaped intertwining branches can be mesmerizing. In my sister's garden, it is magnificent with early-blooming tulips planted in front—both catch the late-afternoon sun beautifully. Aiming a light into the branches allows her to enjoy the unique character of this shrub throughout the night. In early spring, twisted catkins appear followed by contorted, round light green leaves.

A mature Harry Lauder's walking stick can grow to 10 feet tall with a 13-foot spread, but it takes a long time to reach maturity. Because of its slow growth habit, it is very valuable for small gardens. It will grow in full sun to moderately deep shade in any type of soil and is hardy to Zone 6.

CORKSCREW WILLOW (DRAGON-CLAW WILLOW)— SALIX MATSUDANA 'TORTUOSA'

THE GRAY-GREEN, tortuously twisted branches of the corkscrew willow are most impressive uplighted or silhouetted against a white or pale background.

Like the Harry Lauder's walking stick, this small tree is best appreciated in the evening garden when it is leafless. A light dusting of snow on the branches adds another dimension to its contorted beauty. The corkscrew willow should stand alone where you can get a good look at it.

In spring, this willow produces inconspicuous catkins. The 3- to 6-inch-long gray-green leaves turn a lovely shade of gold in autumn.

As a young tree, it has a pyramidal shape and grows slowly. As it matures, it grows faster and spreads out to 20 feet or more. However, this willow can easily be kept small with judicious pruning. The intriguing gnarled form of the branches make the prunings interesting in flower arrangements.

Grow the corkscrew willow in full sun or light shade in any type of soil. It is hardy to Zone 5.

Textured Bark

Paper bark maple, **above,** *and white birch,* **opposite,** *provide year-round visual interest.*

THIS GROUP, like the Sculpture & Silhouette plants, is especially important in an evening garden for year-round enjoyment. These plants are of interest for their textured or colored bark.

The bark of most trees and shrubs is often ignored, as the eye is caught by the foliage or flowers. However, in winter, when deciduous plants have lost their leaves, it is the bark that makes them attractive. A few trees have such unique bark that they are welcome sights year-round.

Unless the bark is white, like that of the paper birch, which can easily grab your attention at night, the tree should be illuminated in the evening garden. Depending on the technique and type of bark, the effect can be subtle or dramatic.

Experiment with lighting before you install the fixtures. Most bark is well displayed by uplighting—shining a spotlight or floodlight up from the base of the tree. Also experiment with the distance the light is placed from the trunk and the intensity of

the light. If a tree has roughly textured bark, grazing light—where several lights just brush the surface from different angles—is the most effective technique for highlighting contours.

STRIPED MAPLE (MOOSEWOOD)— ACER PENSYLVANICUM

THE WHITE-STRIPED VEINING on the trunk and branches of this tree make it outstanding in an

evening garden, especially in winter when the foliage does not distract the viewer. The striped maple is one of the snake-bark maples, so named for the longitudinal lines up the trunk and along the branches that resemble the slightly scaly stripes on a snake.

This is a small tree, growing 15 to 20 feet tall, with a short trunk and an open crown of upright branches. It often grows in shrub form. The new shoots and branches are bright green, aging to gray-green with characteristic white-striped veining. The three-lobed leaves turn clear yellow in the fall and are magnificent in the light of the setting sun.

In general, maples will grow in any rich, well-drained soil and need a climate that gets at least 30 inches of rain a year. Maples respond well to pruning and training. In periods of drought, water thoroughly at least once every two weeks. Fertilize once a year.

The striped maple grows best in full sun and tolerates a range of soil types, but it will not grow in very alkaline soil. Striped maple is native to the northeastern United States and the Appalachian Mountains. It is hardy from Zone 3 to 7.

PAPERBARK MAPLE—
ACER GRISEUM

To FULLY APPRECIATE a paperbark maple in the evening garden, plant it where you can get close to it. When softly illuminated, the convolutions of the peeling bark are fascinating. Night or day, its appeal

is its papery cinnamon-brown bark that curls back, separating into thin sheets, revealing a golden brown underskin. In autumn, the leaves turn bright red and orange—they are gorgeous in the late-afternoon sun.

The paperbark maple branches low on the main stem, only 3 or 4 feet above ground. It is a slow-growing tree that will reach 20 feet tall. New growth is slightly fuzzy.

Like the striped maple, the paperbark maple will languish in alkaline soil, but flourishes in any well-drained soil that is amended with organic material. It requires a minimum of 30 inches of rain a year and is hardy from Zone 5 to 8.

CANOE BIRCH
(PAPER BIRCH)—
BETULA PAPYRIFERA

EVERY EVENING GARDENER who can should consider the canoe birch. Even if not illuminated, the brilliant white bark is striking on moonlit nights.

The canoe birch is the native white birch of eastern North America. It can grow up to 90 feet tall in the wild, but in cultivation it rarely exceeds 30 feet. This tree flowers in late winter to early spring with 3- to 4-inch-long catkins, followed by conelike fruits in autumn. The leaves turn a lovely clear yellow in the fall—another plus for the evening garden.

Birch are often planted in clumps of three. Allow at least 24 inches between trees. Plant balled and burlapped or container-grown trees in early spring. Mulch well and water thoroughly. Once established, birch trees do not transplant easily.

If you have restrictions on water usage, do not plant birch, as they need to be kept well watered. Beware that when stressed from lack of water, canoe birch is subject to bronze birch borer, which may cause the loss of the tree.

Birch trees grow in most types of well-drained soil, as long as they are kept moist. The canoe birch is hardy from Zone 3 to 7.

RIVER BIRCH (RED BIRCH)—
BETULA NIGRA

THE RIVER BIRCH IS STUNNING in the evening garden with lights illuminating its reddish-brown bark. Even when the tree is in leaf, there is enough bark visible to make this of interest year-round.

I first saw a river birch at a friend's property, near where I parked my car. The bark had a handsome reddish shine from the light of the headlights. I suggested that he feature the tree at night, and the next day we installed low-voltage, variable-focus floodlights. He enjoys changing the intensity of the lighting so that the tree always looks different.

'Heritage' is an attractive river birch cultivar with dark green leaves and salmon-white bark—perfect for the evening garden, even without illumination. The salmon tinge to the bark makes it outstanding at sunset.

Grow river birch in the same manner as canoe birch. The river birch, which reaches a height of 60 to 80 feet, is hardy from Zone 5 to 10.

RED-BARKED DOGWOOD
(TATARIAN DOGWOOD)—
CORNUS ALBA

This shrub is grown for its handsome red stems that make a striking statement when illuminated not only in an evening garden, but in a winter garden as well. When young, the stems are almost upright; they arch at maturity. The dark green leaves with red veins are slightly silvered underneath, making them attractive when viewed and illuminated from below. In spring, large, flat clusters of off-white flowers add to this shrub's allure.

For the evening garden, I especially like the variegated cultivated hybrid 'Elegantissima.' It has all the attributes of the red-barked dogwood, but is particularly appealing

When illuminated, the stems of red-barked dogwood, **left**, *make a striking statement.* **Right:** *river birch.*

Textured Bark

for its leaves with broad white margins and mottled inner sections.

Plant this dogwood in full sun to medium shade. Prune severely in spring to maintain a strong winter color and a stem height between 5 and 6 feet.

The red-barked dogwood grows well in any type of soil, as long as it is moist. It thrives even in waterlogged soil. It is hardy to Zone 5.

YELLOW-TWIG DOGWOOD—
CORNUS STOLONIFERA
'FLAVIRAMEA' (C. SERICEA
'FLAVIRAMEA')

Whether planted alone or with red-barked dogwood, the yellow-green branches of

this shrub are an unusual and welcome touch of color in the late afternoon and evening winter garden. The pale-colored stems need little illumination to be visible at night, especially in a snowy landscape.

The yellow-twig dogwood sports light to mid-green elliptic leaves that turn yellow in the fall, blending well with the branches. The leaves in autumn are vibrant in the late-afternoon sun.

Like the red-barked dogwood, yellow-twig dogwood thrives in moist soil in full sun or partial shade. In spring, before it sends out new growth, a severe pruning will help keep the shrub within bounds and improve winter color. It is hardy to Zone 5.

Flowers Aglow at Sunset

Glory-of-the-snow, **above,** *in early spring.* **Opposite:** *Wood hyacinth and forget-me-nots.*

WHEN I SEE a garden in the lengthening light at the end of the day, I am reminded of the Gilbert and Sullivan operetta *Trial by Jury.* In one song, a judge is reminiscing. As a struggling young lawyer, he became tired of the poor life and fell in love with a rich attorney's ugly elderly daughter. The rich attorney was pleased to have made a match for her and cajoled the young lawyer, saying, "She may very well pass for 43 in the dusk with the light behind her." Indeed, it is a most flattering light, for plants and people alike.

Look out into the garden in the late afternoon and you will see that something magical occurs that sets off certain colors of flowers to perfection. Although they may be attractive during the day, these blooms take on a rosy glow and almost fluoresce in the waning light at sunset.

When planning your evening garden, it is important to consider the direction from which light will shine on it. Obviously, a west-facing garden can capture the last rays of sun to perfection. I have chosen a range of plants whose colors react most favorably to the late light. A pleasant array of colors awaits your palette—yellows, reds, mauves, greens and blues.

PEACH-LEAVED BELLFLOWER—CAMPANULA PERSICIFOLIA

THE BLUE FLOWERS of this bellflower become almost

electric in the late-afternoon sun. What a sight to see—the 1½-inch bell-shaped flowers do not hang, but rather stand out horizontally along the top portion of the 2- to 3-foot stems. Elegant by day, they are spectacular in the late afternoon. Although they can be illuminated at night, the magic cannot be captured by artificial light.

Place this hardy perennial near the front of a border where it can catch the sun's rays when it blooms in early summer. Hardy to Zone 4, it grows best in moist soil in full sun to partial shade. To promote a second bloom, remove faded flowers.

GLORY-OF-THE-SNOW— CHIONODOXA LUCILIAE

EACH YEAR, I anticipate the days in early spring when I can walk down to the water at sunset and watch the late afternoon sun catch a west-facing hillside planted with glory-of-the-snow and yellow daffodils. Together, they turn the hillside a luminous, almost cobalt blue dotted with a few splashes of yellow.

Glory-of-the-snow is a showy early-spring-blooming bulb, perfectly suited to the evening garden. The 1-inch star-shaped flowers bloom in a small cluster. The vibrant blue flowers with white centers face upward, adding delicate points of white to the garden later in the evening. There can be great variation in the flowers—the white center may be tiny or almost obliterate the blue.

Glory-of-the-snow's leaves are grasslike, growing to about 4 inches long, but the flowers are the attention-grabbers of this bulb. The plants set seed and naturalize freely, increasing in number year after year.

Plant bulbs in autumn 3 inches deep and 3 inches apart in good, well-drained soil. Mulch with compost or well-rotted manure. Keep lightly moist during the growing season. This flower is hardy to Zone 4.

PINK TURTLEHEAD— CHELONE LYONII

I HAVE LONG ADMIRED pink turtlehead for its unusual flowers that do look exactly as their name implies. A bonus is that it blooms in late summer, when my perennial border can look a bit tired.

Last summer, I was visiting a garden in the late afternoon. The lengthening rays of the sun were catching the side of an old barn, weathered to a nondescript gray. In front of the barn, a bed of pink turtleheads were suffused with the warm color from the sun. I have never seen the flower look so beautiful.

Pink turtlehead grows up to 3 feet

The blue of Campanula persicifolia becomes almost electric in the late-afternoon sun.

The magenta colors of cineraria stand out from sweet woodruff and baby's breath. At dark, the cineraria becomes invisible.

tall, with 1-inch rose-purple flowers stemming from a compact terminal spike. The flowers are related to snapdragons and have two lips. The upper lip is arched and notched—the similarity to a turtle's beak is remarkable.

Turtleheads grow best in partial shade and prefer rich, humusy soil that is kept evenly moist. They are hardy to Zone 4.

CINERARIA—
SENECIO X HYBRIDUS

I ALWAYS THOUGHT of cineraria as a greenhouse plant until I visited a friend's home in northern California where I saw it used in a garden. In the middle of a lush green bed of sweet woodruff and baby's breath was a magenta cineraria. I went back out to the garden late in the day and was awestruck by the cineraria, fluorescing in the garden. Within 15 minutes, the daylight had faded entirely and the cineraria was barely visible.

Cineraria flowers resemble chrysanthemums, but the leaves are a dead giveaway—they are large (up to 4 inches in diameter), bright to deep green, lobed and with slightly toothed edges. The 2-inch flower heads are borne in broadly branching clusters. The flower colors vary but are often seen in white, reddish-pink, blue or magenta, sometimes with contrasting colored rings. The reddish-pink and magenta flowers take on a special glow in the late afternoon.

Cineraria is not easy to grow from seed, but you can buy plants that are in bud or just beginning to bloom and plant them outside. Plants bought in full bloom do not adapt readily to life outdoors, but they can make lovely houseplants. Cineraria can be grown outdoors only in the coastal areas of California.

CLEMATIS

WHILE I WAS still a daytime-only gardener, I joined the ranks of those who believe that clematis is the "Queen of Climbers." They are equally regal in the early evening garden. With over 100 named cultivars, and with flowers in a variety of sizes, shapes and colors, they are unbeatable plants when trained on a trellis or arbor.

Flowers range from large saucers to dainty bells. Choose varieties that are pink, cerise or purple for a vibrant late-afternoon glow.

'Ville de Lyon' has 5-inch velvety carmine flowers on 10- to 12-foot vines.

'Nelly Moser' has pale pink petals and a central stripe of deep pink. The huge 7- to 9-inch flowers bloom profusely in May and June and often repeat in September.

Clematis x *jackmanii* (Jackman clematis) was the first large-flowered hybrid developed and is still popular.

In the evening, clematis live up to their reputation as "Queen of Climbers." Above, Clematis 'Carnaby'; opposite, Clematis 'John Warren.'

The abundant purple flowers, 4 to 6 inches in diameter, bloom from July to October.

If you include white flowering varieties like 'Henryi' or 'Duchess of Edinburgh' and sweet autumn clematis (*C. maximowicziana*), the queen will reign in the evening garden throughout the summer.

Clematis prefer rich, moist, well-drained, slightly alkaline soil. Choose a location that allows the vines full sun but keeps the roots shaded and cool. Plant the crown 2 to 3 inches deep and cover with soil. Mulch well with organic material. Fertilize once during the growing season. Depending on the variety, it is hardy from Zone 4 to 10.

COLEUS—COLEUS X HYBRIDUS

SOME PEOPLE dismiss coleus as too common, but these annuals should be reconsidered. Coleus with pink or yellow to chartreuse leaves are the choice for their vibrance in the late afternoon and into the evening. 'Bellingrath Pink' has a lovely combination of shades.

Coleus like shaded or semishaded areas. The leaves range in size from ½ inch to 3 inches, depending on the variety, and may be scalloped or fringed. Plants range from 18 to 30 inches high. New dwarf varieties grow no more than 10 inches high. The 'Fashion Parade' series has particularly bold coloration.

Often coleus are not labeled when you buy them. If you see a plant you like, buy it and eventually you can take cuttings from your plant to increase your collection. Cuttings easily root in water or light soil. Just dip the ends in rooting hormone. For bushier plants, pinch off flower buds as they appear.

JAPANESE BLOOD GRASS— IMPERATA CYLINDRICA 'RED BARON'

THE BLOOD-RED COLOR of this grass is a showstopper in the early evening garden, if it is planted so that the late-afternoon sun can backlight it. This grass is prized for both its form and, especially, its coloration. At the base of the clump, each blade of grass is a medium green; several inches up, the blade changes to red. It only grows to 20 inches tall and has a very upright habit. For the most eye-catching display, plant it in groups of three or more in the foreground of a border.

Japanese blood grass prefers rich, moist, well-drained soil. It gives its best color in partial shade, with at least several hours of full sun each day. It is hardy to Zone 5.

CARDINAL FLOWER— LOBELIA CARDINALIS

MY SISTER-IN-LAW grows this perennial, and by chance she planted it in the best possible location—at the west-facing edge of a woodland. The late-afternoon sun catches the vibrant red flowers and sets them aglow. The contrast of the

ALTHOUGH YOU MAY overlook grape hyacinth because it is common, take another look at this spring-blooming bulb in the late-afternoon light, when the blue flowers snap to life. Thirty to forty ½-inch drooping urn-shaped flowers are clustered along the top portion of a leafless stalk, resembling miniature bunches of grapes. I have clusters of them planted around the uprights of a split-rail fence that winds up a hill. They take over the job of glorifying the late afternoon after the glory-of-the-snow has faded into memory.

In the fall, plant bulbs 3 inches deep and 3 inches apart in an area where you can appreciate their delicate fragrance. Grape hyacinth is most effective in large groupings, so don't be afraid to plant 25 or more bulbs in a natural-looking swath. Avoid planting in rows. The narrow leaves appear in the fall; in spring, deep blue flowers bloom.

Grape hyacinth grows best in full sun in deep, rich, somewhat sandy soil that is well-drained. It is hardy to Zone 5.

PETUNIA—
PETUNIA X HYBRIDA

EVEN THOUGH PETUNIAS are one of the most commonly grown summer-blooming annuals, they need to be elevated to the status of one of the best annuals for an evening garden. Last year, I grew

dark woods behind accentuates this effect. Cardinal flowers are excellent summer-blooming perennials that range in height from 3 to 6 feet tall. Hardy to Zone 3, they grow best in moist soil in a semishaded location, but will tolerate sun. Plant in rich, moist soil and keep them mulched year-round. They self-seed freely.

BEE BALM (OSWEGO TEA,
RED BERGAMOT)—
MONARDA DIDYMA

THE ROBUST RED COLOR of this native American herb is exquisite in the light of late afternoon. Bee balm is a distinctive perennial, growing 2 to 3 feet tall, that has square stems and opposite leaves. It has a large ragged head of bright crimson flowers and reddish bracts, which make it a good choice to plant in a perennial border. Plant it in front of a white fence or white flowers to show it off to its fullest.

Monarda fistulosa, or wild bergamot, is distinguished by its pinkish or pale lavender flowers with lilac-tinged bracts that glow in the early evening.

To get the largest blooms, bee balm should not be allowed to flower the first year. Just keep cutting back any flower heads as they form. In the second and subsequent years, cut the flower heads back after they bloom and you may have a second flowering in the fall. After a killing frost, cut back the stalks almost to ground level and mulch the plant well. In spring, remember to remove the mulch.

Bee balm grows best in partial shade to full sun in rich, moist soil. It is hardy to Zone 4.

The common petunia is one of the best annuals for the evening garden. **Left:** *Petunia* x *hybrida 'White Cascade.' A Shirley poppy,* **right**, *at sunset.*

'Red Star,' whose coloration looks like a white star on a red background. In the late afternoon, the red glowed. As the light dimmed, the red portion faded, leaving a bold white star. What a superb flower.

With hybridization has come great variation in the funnel-shaped flowers, which range from 2 to 4 inches in diameter. Some are fringed, some double, still others have wavy edges. The colors range from white to pink, red, purple, blue and yellow, and have striping, barring or other markings.

Grandiflora petunias have the largest, frilliest flowers. The multiflora petunias are not so showy, but they have the advantage of disease resistance. Choose several different petunias and see how they react in the changing light as the day progresses from afternoon to evening.

Small plants may be purchased at nurseries and garden centers in early summer. Petunias can also be grown from seed by those who start the seed indoors at least eight weeks before the last frost date. Transplant outdoors after all danger of frost has passed, allowing 12 inches between plants.

Keep petunias well watered during hot weather. After the first flush of bloom, cut the plants back and feed them to encourage new growth and flowering.

SHIRLEY POPPY— PAPAVER RHOEAS

ALTHOUGH THEY MAY be difficult to grow, a mass planting of Shirley poppies is awesome at sunset. The poppies are usually grown as a mixture of white, pink, rose, salmon and scarlet flowers. The 2-inch blooms appear to be made of crepe paper, with their slightly crin-kled petals, but will withstand rain better than some of the other poppies.

Shirley poppies are hardy spring-blooming annuals that grow 2 or 3 feet high and have branching, wiry stems. Like most poppies, they prefer cool weather. Poppies do not transplant well. Sow seeds outdoors in fall or early spring in full sun and well-drained soil.

Bright Flowers

*Beautiful by day, marigolds, **above**, and daffodils, **opposite**, hold their own as night falls.*

I LIKE TO THINK of this group of bright flowers as transition plants that gloriously usher the garden from day into night. Their brilliant colors tend to look good in the midday sun, but the lingering rays at sunset show them off to perfection.

Pale yellows hold their own when night sets in. The stronger yellows and oranges benefit from the addition of soft lighting after dark and will then continue to brighten the garden all night long.

When planning your evening garden, also consider golden and pale orange flowers, like the humble goldenrod or the stalwart gloriosa daisy, that can make the early-evening garden come alive. The black-eyed susan vine is perfect, trailing along the ground or up a trellis or arbor, with its sightless black eyes that blend with the dark of night. Nasturtiums, with their flowers in varying shades of orange and yellow, are magnificent in the early-evening garden.

SWEET SULTAN
'DAIRY MAID'—
AMBERBOA MOSCHATA SSP.
SUAVEOLENS (CENTAUREA
MOSCHATA SSP. SUAVEOLENS)

U SUALLY WHEN I introduce a new plant into my garden, it is one that I have seen somewhere else and admired, or a new hybrid of a tried and true plant. On occasion, I come across a plant in a catalog whose description leaps out at me as perfect for a particular spot. Such was the case with sweet sultan 'Dairy Maid.' It sounded ideal for my early evening garden, and it was.

Legend has it that in the early seventeenth century, the sultan of Constantinople saw *Centaurea moschata* in flower during his travels in the Middle East. He brought home seeds, and soon it was in cultivation in Turkey. His countrymen named the flower sweet sultan in honor of him. 'Dairy Maid' is a new variety.

This vibrant, fragrant annual is only recently available in commerce. It grows 18 to 24 inches high and bears 2-inch sunflower-yellow flowers in summer.

Evening gardeners favor Exbury hybrid azaleas, **top. Bottom:** *A canna.*

It grows best in full sun and well-drained soil. Be sure to locate it so that it catches the late-afternoon sun.

EXBURY HYBRID AZALEAS
(KNAP HILL AZALEAS)
RHODODENDRON CV.

ALL EVENING gardeners should consider growing Exbury hybrid azaleas. They are a flamboyant group of azaleas with large flowers up to 3 inches wide in pastel hues of orange, yellow, peach and red not seen in any other group of azaleas. Exburies are among the last of the azaleas to bloom—usually in late May or early June—and they give the season a marvelous send-off. Their sweet fragrance persists into the early evening.

There is something about seeing them in bloom and inhaling their sweet fragrance that always puts me in an exuberant mood. When I designed a garden around a swimming pool, I was quick to plant several Exbury azaleas where they would catch the late-afternoon sun and also be illuminated by the nearby post lights.

The large flowers are borne in small trusses on shrubs up to 4 feet tall. Their colors and sweet fragrance are truly remarkable. Unlike many other azaleas, they are deciduous, so they are not of interest during the winter.

Grow azaleas in full sun or partial shade in well-drained acidic soil that contains a high percentage of organic matter. Mulch well to conserve moisture. Prune, if necessary, immediately

after the plants bloom, or you'll risk cutting off the next year's flower buds. They are hardy to Zone 5.

CANNA—
CANNA X GENERALIS

CANNA 'WYOMING' has been the cornerstone of my garden for 14 years, radiant in the sunset every summer. It was serendipity that made me plant the showy, bright golden-orange flowered canna with bronze-red foliage just past the corner of the house, where it gets the late-afternoon sun. I am basically a lazy gardener, and I never dig up the bulbs to overwinter them in the basement as I should. But that particular spot must be a warm microclimate within my garden, because the glorious canna comes back year after year.

Cannas are among the showiest of the summer-blooming bulbs. They grow from 3 to 6 feet tall with very large leaves that unfurl from the base of the stem. Much hybridization has given rise to a range of colors in the leaves. Some of the best hybrids for evening enjoyment include 'City of Portland,' which grows 3½ feet tall with green leaves and rosy-pink flowers that glow in the evening. 'Richard Wallace' gets 3 to 4 feet tall and has green leaves with golden-yellow flowers. 'Pfitzer's Primrose Yellow' is only 30 inches tall with green leaves and lovely, soft barium-yellow flowers.

Plant canna bulbs in the spring after all danger of frost has passed and the soil has warmed to about 65

At night, the pale yellow daisylike flowers of Coreopsis verticillata 'Moonbeam' appear to float in the air above the green leaves.

degrees F—the same time you transplant tomatoes into your garden. Select a sunny location with moist, rich soil. After frost (except in Zones 8 and south), dig up clumps and store in a cellar or frost-free but cool area.

THREADLEAF COREOPSIS— COREOPSIS VERTICILLATA 'MOONBEAM'

EVEN ITS NAME implies that this perennial should be considered for inclusion in your evening garden. At night, the dainty 2-inch flowers appear to float in the air, well above the narrow green leaves. Although the pale yellow daisylike flowers almost cover the plant in midsummer, forming an 18- to 24-inch bushy mound, there is an ethereal quality to the plant. Threadleaf coreopsis is

a lovely low-maintenance perennial that will keep blooming almost until frost.

Coreopsis grows best in full sun to partial shade. It prefers dry, well-drained soil, but can grow in most garden soils. Divide plants in spring or fall. Coreopsis is hardy to Zone 4.

LEOPARD'S BANE— DORONICUM CORDATUM

THE BRIGHT YELLOW, narrow-petaled, daisylike flowers of leopard's bane add a bright, sunny touch to even the dreariest spring evening. Leopard's bane grows 1 to 2½ feet tall. The single 2-inch yellow flower heads are borne on thin stalks with inconspicuous alternate leaves. The flower heads have a single row of ray flowers.

Leopard's bane grows best in partial shade, especially in hot climates, or it will go dormant. It prefers rich, moist soil and is hardy to Zone 4.

RED HOT POKER (TORCH LILY)—KNIPHOFIA UVARIA

RED HOT POKER makes a strong statement in the summer evening garden with its flowers that look like brightly hued exclamation points. The flowers are borne tightly in 6- to 12-inch-long showy clusters atop sturdy 2- to 6-foot spikes. The flowers open from the lower portion of the cluster to the top, extending bloom over a long period. It is a striking plant, especially in a group of 7 to 12.

One of the more commonly grown varieties has red-orange

blooms near the top with pale yellow flowers below, so it looks like a poker that was once white hot (yellow portion) and is cooling to red hot at its tip. Other cultivated varieties have spikes with yellow, orange, scarlet or coral flowers.

Plant red hot poker in full sun in an area with moist, well-drained soil. In winter, tie the leaves into a bundle to protect the crown from excess moisture, or dig up the rhizomes and replant them in the spring. It is hardy to Zone 5.

STATICE— LIMONIUM SINUATUM

My husband has grown statice in his garden for many years, using it for dried flower wreaths and arrangements. In the garden, the flowers are long-lasting—perfect for the lazy gardener who may not get out to cut them for several weeks.

Statice is a colorful summer-blooming annual that grows 12 to 30 inches tall. It thrives in warm weather. The leaves are somewhat tufted and are positioned at ground level. The small ½-inch flowers are borne on clusters of three to five winged branches. With repeated cutting, the plants will bloom all summer.

Start seeds indoors in peat pots about eight weeks before the last frost date in spring. Transplant outdoors when all danger of frost has passed and the soil has warmed to about 65 degrees F. Statice does not transplant well if the plants are too large.

Grow statice in full sun and well-drained sandy soil. Statice is tolerant of heat and drought.

Kniphofia makes a bold statement in the summer.

DAFFODILS—NARCISSUS SP.

Daffodils are unquestionably one of the best flowers for any spring garden, and more so for any spring evening garden. I always feel that spring has actually arrived when the first of the tall daffodils blooms, and that is cause for celebration.

The earlier blooming bulbs, like snowdrops, crocuses and even the small species of daffodils, are heralds of spring—announcing that the real thing is on its way. However, the possibility still lurks of winter creeping back in and dropping another several inches of snow. But once these beautiful large daffodils start to bloom, I feel that the warm weather is here to stay. My celebration can range from an occasional party thrown on the spur of the moment to a solitary toast by me to Mother Nature for providing such beauty to usher in a new season of growth and renewal.

Several springs ago, when I arrived home well after dark, a bright patch of yellow was there to greet me next to my front door. I saluted the first daffodils of the year, and then began planning for more daffodils in the garden next year in areas where they could be appreciated at night.

Daffodils can be the base around which the rest of the spring evening garden is planned. Between species and hybrids, there are so many different varieties that, here on Long Island, one type of daffodil or another is in bloom from midwinter through May. From the tiny *Narcissus asturiensis*, which is only 4 to 5 inches tall with proportionately diminutive flowers, that blooms in late January or early February, to the fragrant 18-inch poet's narcissus, also known as pheasant's eye, or *N. poeticus*, that blooms in May, there is a broad range of daffodils that will fill an evening garden with their beauty throughout the spring.

Choose from single or double

flowers and a range of petal and cup colors, from white through every shade of yellow into orange and pink. One of my new favorites is a creamy iridescent white, fragrant butterfly or split corona daffodil called 'Cassata,' which has a special place in my Crescent Moon garden.

Plant bulbs outdoors in fall at least one month before a hard frost. In warm areas, do not plant until the soil has cooled to below 70 degrees F. Daffodils prefer full sun, but will grow in partial shade. A good rule of thumb is to plant bulbs at a depth that is twice the height of the bulb, allowing at least one bulb-width between them.

Plant in well-drained soil that has been enriched with organic matter. Each fall, mulch with compost or well-rotted manure. Most daffodils are hardy from Zone 4 to 7.

ORANGE CONEFLOWER— RUDBECKIA FULGIDA 'GOLDSTURM STRAIN'

YOU MAY NOT THINK of the adjective "sunny" to describe flowers in an evening garden. However, the plants that fit this description easily make the transition from day to evening. Orange coneflower is a prime example of such a plant. It is a showy summer-blooming perennial that shines in the early evening garden. The sunny, deep golden-yellow 3- to 4-inch flowers are handsomely set off by a bronze-black central cone. They grow 2 to 3 feet tall and have somewhat hairy leaves and stems. Not only does this flower provide bright color in the late afternoon and evening, but it is also excellent as a cut flower.

Orange coneflower does not grow true from seed. However, small plants are readily available in nurseries and garden centers. This flower grows best in full sun or partial shade and will tolerate most soils. Space plants 12 to 15 inches apart. They are hardy to Zone 4.

With its deep golden-yellow flowers, rudbeckia is one plant that shines in the summer garden both day and night.

MARIGOLD—TAGETES SP.

AMONG THE CHEERIEST of the summer-blooming annuals, with their many hues of orange and red, marigolds are the quintessential

Marigolds bloom from spring to frost.

plants for making the transition from day to night in the garden. With little effort, they provide an abundance of color from late spring until frost.

Ten years ago, I planted a large grouping of French marigolds near the swimming pool to bridge the area between the perennial ornamental grasses and the deck. It was more of a success than I could have hoped for. During the day, they were lovely; at sunset, they picked up the last rays of sun and seemed to hold onto the light until after dark. At night, they brightened an otherwise dark corner, adding a bit of their own sunshine.

After the plants died in the autumn, it was easy to pull them out

or rake them away. Imagine my surprise the following spring when I saw tiny plants growing in the gravel. The marigolds had seeded themselves.

The second year's show was better than the first. Marigolds as a rule are hybrids, so seed that is set by the plant will not grow true. In this case, the resulting plants were a delightful mixture of colors and forms with a more natural look than the original planting. They continued to self-seed year after year, until one year when we had a very warm spell in February. The seeds must have sprouted and were then killed by a hard frost. So, in May, I began the cycle again with new plants.

Each of the three marigold species has distinctive characteristics. The African, or Aztec, marigold, *T. erecta*, has the largest flower heads—2 to 6 inches wide. The plants grow 18 to 36 inches high and are well branched, resembling a small bush. The flowers often look like pom-poms in varying shades of yellow and orange. Newer introductions include white (more like a pale greenish-yellow) and mahogany red. The vibrant yellows are especially suited for an evening garden and are effective in an annual border or a foundation planting.

French marigolds, or *T. patula*, grow to 18 inches high. The 2- to 3-inch flower heads have yellow rays often marked with red. Color is more diverse in the hybrids, ranging from pure yellow to red-orange. Many are doubles or have crested flowers. They are perfect edging plants.

Signet, or dwarf, marigolds, *T. tenuifolia*, grow up to 12 inches tall. Among the most attractive are the single 'Lemon Gem' and 'Tangerine Gem.' Both have somewhat lacy foliage that is an attractive foil for the brightly colored 1-inch flowers.

Many types of marigolds are readily available in late spring at nurseries and garden centers as 2- to 4-inch transplants. But marigolds are easily grown from seed. Sow directly outdoors two to three weeks before the last frost date, allowing at least 2 inches between seeds.

Marigolds prefer rich soil and full sun. In the hottest areas of the country, plant them where they will get afternoon shade. Remove spent flowers to encourage continued blooming.

TULIP—TULIPA SP.

YOU MAY WONDER at the choice of tulips as bright flowers. Despite the fact that they close up at night, the outsides of the petals are visible and, depending on the variety, are colorful enough to brightly accent the spring evening garden.

'Court Lady,' for example, is cream with a pale green streak in the center of the petal when closed. Others that you might consider include 'West Point,' a vibrant yellow lily-flowering tulip; 'New Design,' with sunset pink and yellow petals and a white margin on the leaves; 'Mount Tacoma,' a bright white peony-flowered tulip; 'Sweet Harmony,' with lovely lemon petals edged in ivory; and the classic 'Yellow Emperor.'

Tulips are available in many colors and designs—from vibrant reds to stately ivories, from pure colors to mottled ones, with petals edged in contrasting colors or striped down the center. With so many tulips to choose from, you can have varieties that bloom from late winter throughout the spring.

Tulips are probably the most popular and widely planted of all bulbs in cultivation. There are more than 100 species of tulips, and there have been thousands of cultivated varieties grown around the world. Some of the species are small and grow close to the ground, with petals no more than 1 inch long. Hybrid varieties can grow to more than 24 inches tall, with flowers that open fully and measure more than 8 inches across.

In all areas except Zones 8 to 10, tulips can be planted from September until the ground begins to freeze. They should be planted at least 4 to 6 inches deep. Planting them 8 to 10 inches deep, however, results in hardier plants that will come back year after year. Plant 4 to 6 inches apart. Cover with soil and water well. Once the ground has frozen, mulch over the planting. In spring, the leaves will appear, followed by the flowers.

In the warmer climatic zones, tulips need to be precooled. They can be purchased precooled from suppliers, or they can be put in the

Even though they close at night, some white- and light-colored tulips can still accent the spring evening garden.

refrigerator for at least 10 weeks. Be sure not to have apples or pineapples in the refrigerator, as both emit ethylene gas which inhibits bulb growth. After chilling, usually in January or February, plant the bulbs in a cool, semishady location.

ZINNIA—ZINNIA LINEARIS (ZINNIA ANGUSTIFOLIA)

THIS CHARMING ANNUAL grows only 12 to 16 inches high, forming bushlike mounds that glow in the sunset. I plant some each year in a whiskey barrel near the cannas. By late summer, their bright yellow daisylike flowers are cascading down to the ground.

Don't confuse this zinnia with the common garden zinnia. *Zinnia linearis* has leaves that are narrow and are not susceptible to mildew like their common garden cousin. This one has flowers up to 1½ inches wide, with a black center and yellow or orange petals. New varieties have off-white flowers.

This zinnia is a great bedding plant in a low-water landscape, as it is extremely drought-tolerant. Whatever time of night or day, *Zinnia linearis* will catch the light of the sun or the moon and shine in the garden.

Allow at least 12 inches between plants and grow in full sun. *Zinnia linearis* will do well in average, well-drained soil.

Not to be confused with the common garden zinnia, Zinnia linearis forms bushlike mounds of flowers that appear to glow in the sunset.

Pale Flowers on the Ground

Low-growing, light-colored flowers such as rose daphne snap to life after dark.

CONSIDER LOW-GROUND plants, or ground covers, with pale flowers for the evening garden. In a traditional day garden, many ground covers are grown for their foliage—their flowers are sometimes just an incidental benefit. Yet in an evening garden, light-colored flowers stand out.

Many pale-colored flowers may be overshadowed by neighboring bright flowers during the day, but they snap to life after dark, in the light of the moon or when illuminated by artifi-cial lighting. As I drive up to the house in late spring, my headlights catch the sweet violets that have come up along the edge of the drive. Once again, these pale gems are a personal reminder to slow down and revel in the beauty around me at night.

Remember that at night, it is the contrast of light and dark that is most important. It may be difficult to distinguish the exact shade and hue of a pale flower; however, the flower will be noticeable.

Some flowers that are included in other categories, such as tulips, petunias, daylilies, evening primrose and campanulas, have varieties that include pale flowers. Keep this in mind as you glance through seed cat-alogs and make up your plant list.

CALAMINT—CALAMINTHA NEPETOIDES (CALAMINTHA NEPETA NEPETA)

CALAMINT, although not a true mint, is a fine addition to your

The flowers of calamint, **top,** *catch the light of the moon.* **Bottom:** *At night, blue star creeper flowers look like tiny stars. In warm areas, the plant makes a graceful perennial ground cover.*

evening garden. The pale lilac or white flowers catch the light of the moon. They are numerous in long clusters along the top portion of the stem. Get closer and look at the unusual two-lipped flowers.

Calamint flowers from summer to early fall, growing 12 to 18 inches tall. The stems are erect with hairy, oval, round-toothed leaves. This compact perennial has an added benefit—when lightly brushed, its foliage releases a delightful minty scent into the air.

Calamint grows best in well-drained soil in full sun. It is becoming more popular and is now available through some mail-order sources. It is hardy from Zone 5 to 10.

BLUE STAR CREEPER— LAURENTIA FLUVIATILIS (ISOTOMA FLUVIATILIS)

WHEN VISITING a friend's California garden, I went out to smell the roses one evening, but got completely sidetracked. On the ground, in the center bed, were hundreds of small flowers that looked like tiny stars that had fallen from the heavens. I was enraptured—my friend eventually came out to see what had happened to me.

Blue star creeper is aptly named. In warm areas, it is a graceful, perennial evergreen ground cover, diminutive in size, with ¼-inch dark green leaves that form a 3-inch-high mat which spreads out to 12 inches. The tiny ¼-inch light blue flowers bloom most profusely in late spring, but in mild areas, the flowers bloom year-round, looking at night like a sprinkling of palest blue on a carpet of green.

Blue star creeper is perfect for a rock garden or on a low wall where it can cascade and be appreciated. It may also be planted between stepping stones.

Blue star creeper prefers rich soil in full sun or partial shade. Allow 6 to 12 inches between plants. Keep it well watered, especially in summer. It is hardy from Zone 9 to 10.

ROSE DAPHNE—
DAPHNE CNEORUM

Rose daphne is another evening plant I have growing near the swimming pool. I enjoy the small evergreen plant at night year-round, contrasted with the light-colored gravel that surrounds it. In the late spring, its 1-inch-long evergreen leaves are joined by clusters of fragrant pink flowers that glimmer in the moonlight and perfume the surrounding air.

Rose daphne has a low, creeping habit. It grows to only 12 inches high and has a tendency to sprawl into a large mat. My original rose daphne, planted eight years ago, is now 24 inches in diameter, yet only 8 inches tall. It is a handsome ground cover along the edge of a wide border or in a rock garden, especially if you contrast it with light-colored mulch or gray foliage plants.

Rose daphne grows best in loose, sandy loam. It prefers neutral or slightly alkaline soil. In the winter, gently cover the plant with evergreen boughs to protect it from winter sun scald. It is hardy to Zone 5.

FIVE SPOT—
NEMOPHILA MACULATA
'FIVE SPOT'

Much of an evening garden is an illusion that you create. This plant is an amusing addition for its own illusion. At the tip of each of the five pale blue petals is a deep blue spot—hence its name. At night, the spots disappear. With a little imagination, you might believe that some nocturnal creature took sym-metrical bites out of each petal.

Five spot is a trailing annual that grows to 12 inches long. The flowers are borne in clusters at the tips of the branches. Less than 2 inches across, the flowers are slightly bell-shaped with deeper blue veins and a dark spot at the petal tips.

A cool-weather wildflower, it grows well in northern and high-altitude gardens. In mild climates, direct-seed it in the garden in fall. In areas with severe winters, sow the

seeds in early spring. Thin plants to 12 inches apart to form a lovely carpet of flowers.

Five spot grows best in full sun to partial shade. It prefers average to dry well-drained soil and performs best when provided with afternoon shade.

GROUND PINK (MOSS PINK)— PHLOX SUBULATA

I REMEMBER GROUND pink in a garden from childhood. When I emptied the garbage after dinner (a chore I did begrudgingly), I would catch a glimpse of the cheery white and pink flowers at the edge of the garden. I believed that during the day, they were there for everyone's enjoyment, but at night, they were my special friends.

Ground pink is a creeping evergreen perennial that is perfect for a rock garden. Plant it between stepping stones, as a ground cover or at the edge of a perennial border. It grows to about 6 inches high, forming a dense mat of small needlelike leaves. Small 1-inch flowers appear in dense clusters and cover the plant each spring. These flowers may be pink, white or bright purple.

Ground pink grows best in average well-drained soil in full sun or partial shade. For a more dense, compact plant, cut back the stems halfway after all the blooms have faded. It is hardy to Zone 4.

Phlox subulata is an ideal perennial for the nighttime rock garden.

Evening Gardens

White Flowers

Among the earliest bloomers, snowdrops grace the late-winter evening garden.

WHITE FLOWERS outshine all others in the evening garden. Even with minimal light they pop into view, while other flowers remain invisible. When I first began a serious study of evening gardens, my inclination was to include only white flowers as I felt safe with anything white. It was a way of taking an adaptation of Vita Sackville-West's famous White Garden at Sissinghurst to the next millennium—using it as a night garden.

There is a special pristine charm to an all-white garden that is absent in other monochromatic gardens. Perhaps it is because white is an absolute.

Over the years, I have become involved in close-up photography. Looking at blowups of certain flowers, I noticed that they appeared iridescent. Perhaps this quality allows for more reflection of the ambient light as I observed that certain white flowers, such as wisteria, moonflowers and a particular unnamed white

clematis I have growing in my garden, glow brighter at night.

Almost any white flower is good for an evening garden, but keep in mind that some flowers close their petals at night. If the undersides of the petals are not white or light-colored, the flower will become invisible.

As you make your selection of white flowers to include in your garden, annual standbys like sweet alyssum and impatiens may be obvious choices, but consider white ageratum and white cosmos as well. Even among the perennials, certain plants readily come to mind—feverfew, phlox, dahlia and white bleeding heart. But don't overlook gooseneck loosestrife , bloodroot or lily-of-the-valley.

With its 6-foot-tall stalks, goatsbeard deserves a prominent position in the evening garden.

Consider white-flowering shrubs such as viburnum, hydrangea and andromeda. Look up at the trees for inspiration—dogwood, serviceberry and magnolias. Examine the sample garden designs in this book and you will no doubt discover new plants and interesting combinations to include in your evening garden.

There are many common and uncommon plants with white flowers. I have selected some common ones that I feel are musts for the evening garden and others that are more unusual and that may be unfamiliar to you.

GOATSBEARD— ARUNCUS DIOICUS

IN THE EVENING, goatsbeard's white flowers look like cascading fireworks at the back of a flower border.

This showy perennial grows 4 to 6 feet tall and sends up flowering stalks in early summer. The small white flowers are borne on thin branches of a wide-spreading, open, showy cluster.

Goatsbeard is so striking when in bloom that it deserves a prominent position in the evening garden. A soft light aimed down at the bloom will enhance its magic.

Goatsbeard grows best in partial shade and rich, moist soil. It is hardy to Zone 4.

SNOW-IN-SUMMER— CERASTIUM TOMENTOSUM

I WAS VISITING a locally well-known azalea garden late one afternoon. What caught my eye as the sun went down was not the mass of garish azaleas that covered a hillside but the dazzle of the white flowers of snow-in-summer planted in the stone wall at the base of the hill.

Snow-in-summer is doubly good for the evening garden—not only does it have beautiful ½-inch white flowers in late spring, but also the foliage forms a lovely white woolly mat that is attractive at night before the flowers open and again after they fade.

This prostrate perennial only grows to 6 inches tall. It is good as a ground cover or as a rock-garden

plant. Like other gray foliage plants, it is drought-tolerant—an excellent choice for gardeners who have to ration water. But this plant is not perfect—it has a tendency to become invasive.

Grow snow-in-summer in full sun in well-drained soil. It is hardy to Zone 4.

KAMCHATKA BUGBANE— CIMICIFUGA SIMPLEX

AT NIGHT, the flowering bugbane stalks look like fairy wands or long, thin, fuzzy tapers of white—a true midsummer night's fantasy. In reality, tiny white flowers grow tightly in a 1- to 3-foot elongated cluster on this 3- to 4-foot-tall perennial.

Another cimicifuga, black snakeroot (*C. racemosa*) grows up to 6 feet tall with a branched showy flower cluster 1 to 3 feet long. It blooms in late summer to early autumn.

Cimicifugas grow best in a woodland environment in moist soil and partial shade. Plants grown in shade get a lot of lovely foliage but few flowers. Amend the soil with leaf mold and well-rotted compost. They are hardy to Zone 4.

DOVE TREE (HANDKERCHIEF TREE)— DAVIDIA INVOLUCRATA

I ONCE ATTENDED a cocktail party thrown specifically to celebrate the blooming of this tree. Lights were aimed high into the crown, illuminating the leaves and branches—

or so the guests assumed. As the guests gazed up into the trees, they saw what looked like the wings of doves. One guest even remarked how tame the birds were not to fly away with the noise of the party. In fact, it is the large white bracts—leaves on either side of the flowers—that give the illusion of doves' wings.

Some people think the bracts look like handkerchiefs, but they obviously have less imagination than the partygoers. It is worth uplighting this tree for the several weeks in late spring that the bracts are showy.

The dove tree is truly unique. It is a deciduous tree, growing to 50 or 60 feet tall with attractive 6-inch oval leaves.

The dove tree should be planted in light shade. It will grow into full sun as it matures. It grows best in rich, deep loam and is hardy from Zone 6 to 8.

COMMON SHOOTING STAR— DODECATHEON MEADIA

As its name implies, this spring-blooming perennial deserves space in the garden for its flowers, which look like a miniature meteorite shower. A cluster of nodding 1-inch flowers on slender stalks arches out from the top of the 1- to 2-foot reddish stalks. The flower color ranges from white to deep rose. For an evening garden, select only white-flowered plants.

Shooting star grows best in rich, well-drained sandy soil heavily amended with organic matter. It prefers partial shade and needs to be kept moist during the growing season, but can be drier when dormant. Prevent water from standing in the crown, in winter especially, as it may prove fatal. It is hardy to Zone 5.

The white flower bracts of the deciduous dove tree appear for several weeks in the late spring.

HEATHER (WINTER-FLOWERING HEATHER)— ERICA HERBACEA (E. CARNEA)

Here on long island, winter is supposed to be a flowerless time of year in the garden, but not if you are growing winter-flowering heather.

I have grown 'Springwood White,' preferring the contrast of the white flowers and the sparkle they add against the dark, barren winter-night landscape. However, after a real winter with snow, I am inclined to add 'Springwood Pink' whose flowers are light enough to show up at night but have enough color to contrast with the white snow.

'Aurea' is another attractive pink-flowering variety with golden leaves that are lovely and bright. Although

'Anna Sparks' flowers are red, and so are not that visible in the dark, the orange and yellow leaves are show-stoppers.

Heather is a small 12-inch-high shrub that is perfect for use in a rock garden or at the edge of a path or border where it will catch your eye. Try to plant it where it will be seen, and where you will not shovel a foot of snow on top of it.

Heather blooms from midwinter to early spring. Half-inch narrow leaves are clustered along the stems. Leaf color varies from dark in winter to lighter in spring, depending on the variety. Small bell-shaped flowers are borne singly but in profusion along the branches.

Heather grows best in slightly acidic soil in very light shade, but it will tolerate full sun. In deeper

shade, it becomes leggy and may not bloom. Prune lightly after flowering to encourage new flowering shoots for the next year. It is highly susceptible to drought, so keep it well mulched and watered during the summer. It is hardy to Zone 6.

DWARF FOTHERGILLA (DWARF WITCH ALDER)— FOTHERGILLA GARDENII

With the current trend to take gardening so seriously, worrying whether every last plant will fit in, I say it's time to lighten up and have fun. Dwarf fothergilla is nature's answer.

The first time I saw one at night, I got a fit of the giggles. Seeing what looked like 1-inch bottle brushes floating in the air struck me as hi-

'Springwood White' heather, **above,** *blooms during the barren winter months.* **Right,** *the bottle-brushlike flowers of dwarf fothergilla.*

larious. At first, the person whose garden I was visiting was insulted. I reassured him that it was all right to get joy through laughter from the garden, and within minutes, he saw how funny-looking the plant was and started to laugh along with me.

Dwarf fothergilla is a small shrub that grows up to 3 feet tall with 1- or 2-inch broadly wedge-shaped dark green leaves. The undersides of the leaves are white and hairy—another bonus for the evening gardener. The fragrant white flowers are borne in clusters on 1-inch spikes and resemble a bottle brush. It blooms before the leaves open in early to midspring.

Dwarf fothergilla grows best in well-drained, acidic sandy loam in full sun or partial shade. It is hardy to Zone 5.

GUINEA-HEN FLOWER (CHECKERED LILY, SNAKE'S-HEAD)— FRITILLARIA MELEAGRIS

THIS EARLY SPRING-BLOOMING bulb is not well known in America. I first saw it almost 20 years ago in my English cousin's meadow, glimmering in the moonlight. I have since seen it offered by a number of companies here.

The flower is the captivating feature of this plant. The 1½-inch bell-shaped blossoms are borne singly. A close look reveals a white-on-white checkerboard pattern. Flower color is variable from white to purplish-maroon. Grow this plant in a spot where people can easily get down to

look closely at the flowers, day or night.

Guinea-hen flowers are well-suited for a rock garden, growing 12 to 18 inches tall with a few narrow 3- to 6-inch leaves. In fall, plant the bulbs 4 to 6 inches deep in rich well-drained soil. They prefer full sun or light-dappled shade and are hardy to Zone 4.

the three long outer segments and three shorter inner segments of the flower hang in a bell-like fashion.

Snowdrops are late winter- to early spring-flowering bulbs with several narrow gray-green leaves at the base of each stem. The key to successful culture is to plant the bulbs in groups of 15 to 50 or more—otherwise you won't see

Little known in North America, guinea hen flowers are suited for evening gardens.

SNOWDROPS— GALANTHUS NIVALIS

WHAT A JOY IT IS to sit at the dinner table and gaze out into the late-winter garden and see the little white snowdrops bobbing their heads in the moonlight. Although it may still feel like winter, they are a sign that spring will soon arrive. The flowers are unique—at the top of the 3- to 6-inch stem is a rounded protuberance from which

them out there at night. They are quick to multiply and naturalize in the garden. Plant them in several spots where you can also appreciate these beauties from indoors.

In autumn, plant the bulbs 3 inches deep and 3 inches apart. They prefer to be planted in light, rich well-drained soil in full sun. They do well beneath deciduous trees, which are leafless in spring when the bulbs bloom. They are hardy from Zone 3 to 9.

SWEET WOODRUFF—
GALIUM ODORATUM
(ASPERULA ODORATA)

THIS IS AN HERB well suited for evening garden enjoyment. In May, when it is in bloom, take an evening stroll in your garden. Be sure to bring a glass of white wine with you. When you get to the delicate white sweet woodruff flowers, which are easily visible in the moonlight, pick a cluster (and a leaf if you want) and drop them into your glass of wine—instant May wine.

Sweet woodruff is a fragrant, low-growing perennial herb commonly grown as a shade-tolerant groundcover. Native to Europe and Eurasia,

sweet woodruff has become naturalized in some areas of America. The leaves are deep green in whorls of six to eight around the square stem. In midspring, small, sweet-smelling, white funnel-shaped flowers appear in loose clusters.

The foliage has no scent when freshly picked, but soon the sweet aroma of newly mown hay is evident. The scent intensifies as the plant dries. For this reason, it was often strewn in homes and churches to freshen rooms.

Sweet woodruff is slow to germinate from seed; it is usually easier to divide existing clumps to create new plantings. Once established, it will self-seed. It spreads by underground

runners and can become invasive. If your planting gets too large, dig some up and share it with friends.

Sweet woodruff can grow in almost any type of soil, but prefers rich, well-drained loam. It performs equally well in partial to full shade and is hardy to Zone 5.

WHITE GAURA—
GAURA LINDHEIMERI

IN HIS BOOK *The Adventurous Gardener's Sourcebook of Rare and Unusual Plants*, William Mulligan captures the essence of white gaura in an evening garden: "Its magical white flowers hover like a cloud of silvery moths that overnight turn pale pink." The numerous flowers, borne on erect wandlike stalks, easily flutter in the slightest breeze, creating the illusion that each flower is a living creature hovering around the stalk.

Gaura is gaining in popularity, especially with gardeners concerned about water usage. It is a drought-tolerant, bushy summer-blooming perennial that grows to 5 feet high. Start the seed indoors four to six weeks before the last frost date and transplant it outdoors after all danger of frost has passed.

Gaura grows best in full sun in ordinary garden soil. The soil must, however, be well-drained. Water only in the driest part of the summer if there is not sufficient rain.

Once planted, gaura cannot easily be moved as it has a long taproot. It is hardy to Zone 6.

BABY'S BREATH—
GYPSOPHILA PANICULATA

SEVERAL YEARS AGO, I gave my first slide lecture on evening gardens. The final slide in the section on lighting was of holiday lighting that was created to look, I said, like fireworks. The next slide was of baby's breath taken in the evening. I clicked back to the lighting photo— it looked more like an electric imitation of the baby's breath than anything else. Without all the fuss of wiring and with no additional cost to your electric bill, you can easily have the living fireworks in your evening garden by planting baby's breath.

Baby's breath is an airy-looking perennial that grows to 3 feet tall and nearly as wide. In midsummer, the ¼-inch white flowers appear in profusely branched clusters, seeming to burst out all over the plant.

Plant it in a sheltered location, or stake in a windy location. Cut some of the flower sprays before they open and dry them indoors for use in arrangements. Cut back the plant before it goes to seed and you may be rewarded with a second flush of bloom.

For years, I had trouble growing baby's breath until I learned that it will not grow well in rich soil. Baby's breath grows best in full sun in moist, well-drained neutral or slightly alkaline soil. It is hardy to Zone 4.

PERUVIAN DAFFODIL
(ISMENE, BASKET-FLOWER)—
HYMENOCALLIS
NARCISSIFLORA
(PANCRATIUM CALATHINUM,
ISMENE CALATHINA)

WHAT A SURPRISE when you first come across what looks like an 8-inch-long fringed white daffodil in an evening garden. You may be led to it by its sweet scent, although the flowers, especially if softly illuminated, are large enough to be seen from a distance. The exotic summer-blooming bulb is called a Peruvian daffodil. It is a distant cousin of the spring-flowering daffodil—both are members of the amaryllis family.

Peruvian daffodil can reach 2 feet tall, with six to eight upright leaves that grow 2 feet long and 2 inches wide. Plant bulbs 3 inches deep and 6 to 8 inches apart after the soil has warmed in spring. In groups of three or more, these are real attention-grabbers.

These daffodils prefer full sun and well-drained soil. In northern areas, dig up the bulbs in autumn and store indoors for the winter. They are hardy to Zone 8.

CANDYTUFT—
IBERIS SEMPERVIRENS

THE BEST AND SIMPLEST use I have seen of candytuft in an evening garden is as a 2-foot-wide border between a garden and a lawn. Before the candytuft, there were no plants of evening interest in the garden, so at night the garden was as

Striking in appearance, the 8-inch-long flowers of Peruvian daffodils also emit a pleasantly sweet scent.

black as the lawn. For years, people had cut across the lawn at night and had inadvertently stepped into the garden and trampled the plants. Once the candytuft was planted, the delineation between lawn and gar-

den was a bright white swath of flowers that defied crossing.

Candytuft is an evergreen perennial that grows to 12 inches high. The small dark green leaves are on upright stems. In early to late spring, white 1½-inch flowers are borne in lateral finger-shaped clusters, looking like little white tufts above the leaves. Candytuft shines in the evening garden, with or without lighting.

Candytuft grows best in well-drained soil. Do not allow it to dry out completely or it will stop flowering. Prune back after flowering to prevent a center hole in the plant. In cold areas, mulch lightly in the fall to prevent the foliage from browning. It is hardy to Zone 4.

VIRGINIA SWEETSPIRE— ITEA VIRGINICA

I WAS ENCHANTED by the delicacy and novelty of Virginia sweetspire the first time I saw it in a Maryland garden on a summer night. The upright 3- to 6-inch clusters of white flowers rising above the foliage reminded me of a Christmas tree decorated with white candles. The sweet fragrance of the flowers was a jolt back to reality. The flowers, even when cut, are fragrant only at night.

Virginia sweetspire is a 5- to 10-foot deciduous shrub. The upright branches are reddish when young, turning brown as they mature. The flowers are relatively long-lasting. The oval bright green leaves turn brilliant red in autumn, adding interest to the early evening garden even after the flowers have faded.

Virginia sweetspire grows best in moist, well-drained average soil. Although it will tolerate shade, it flourishes in full sun. It is hardy to Zone 5.

SWEET ALYSSUM— LOBULARIA MARITIMA

S WEET ALYSSUM has been a part of every garden I have had since childhood, and it has always been an evening delight. I remember my father and I used to set out the small alyssum plants each spring. As custom dictated, we alternated the

Candytuft, **above**, *makes a good evening border.* **Right:** *Aptly named gooseneck loosestrife blooms all summer long.*

white with the pale lilac variety, placing them 3 or 4 inches apart, envisioning a nice uniform border of alternating colors as the plants grew together.

The alyssum always seemed to have a mind of its own, however, and by summer there would be lovely white mounds with occasional spots of mangy-looking lilac alyssum. On a hot summer night, in my child's imagination, the white alyssum became cool patches of unmelted snow.

When I bent down to touch it, I got a whiff of its honeylike fragrance.

Sweet alyssum grows to 12 inches high. The individual flowers are tiny, borne in clusters only ¾ inch wide. It is excellent in a rock garden or as an edging plant. Try some in a container or window box, where you can get close to catch its aroma.

Sow the seeds directly in the garden in early spring or late summer in a sunny location. If you don't want to start from seed, take into account that only small seedlings transplant well.

Sweet alyssum self-sows, which you can take advantage of if you do not turn the soil every spring. This trait is considered by some a problem, as it tends to seed itself into lawns in warm climates. Personally, I am all for a mixed-ecology ground cover and the less lawn the better.

Sweet alyssum prefers cool weather and will fade a bit in summer, but it perks back up in fall.

GOOSENECK LOOSESTRIFE– LYSIMACHIA CLETHROIDES

GOOSENECK LOOSESTRIFE is aptly named. On a moonlit night, a cluster of the white flower spikes (with their characteristic bend partway up the spike) looks like a gaggle of geese let loose in the garden.

Gooseneck loosestrife grows 2 to 3 feet tall. The small ½-inch white flowers are borne in slender 6- to 8-inch terminal clusters that narrow

With a profusion of white flowers that trail down their branches, spirea deserve a special place in the evening garden.

toward the tip. Unlike many perennials, it blooms for a long period, usually throughout the summer.

Gooseneck loosestrife grows best in sun or partial shade in moist, well-drained soil. It can spread in the garden, especially in moist soil, so you might want to restrict it to a large container. It is hardy to Zone 4.

CUPFLOWER—
NIEREMBERGIA 'MONT BLANC'

T HE SMALL STAR-SHAPED white flowers with a dash of yellow at the center blanket the plant throughout the growing season, making this a perfect bright accent plant in an evening garden. It was chosen as a 1993 All America Seed Winner and the 1993 Fleuroselect Gold Medal Winner. Both awards attest to this plant's reliability and consistency when grown in different areas of the country.

Cupflower is a heat-loving, ground-hugging annual. It grows 5 to 6 inches tall, spreading about 12 inches wide. Evening gardeners can get the best show from this plant by placing it along a border, in a rock garden or as an accent in containers.

It grows best in full sun and well-drained soil. It may be grown from seed if started indoors six to eight weeks before the last frost date. Plant it outdoors after all danger of frost has passed.

SPIREA (BRIDALWREATH)—
SPIRAEA SP.

W ITH THEIR white flowers that seem to trail down their long branches in spring, these lovely small to medium-sized shrubs deserve a special place in the evening garden. Most spireas have white flowers and bloom profusely in the spring. The leaves tend to turn scarlet-orange in autumn, adding interest to the early evening garden even long after the flowers are gone.

If you like the look of small flowers cascading along a branch, there are several different spireas that will fit the bill. Plant more than one variety to add visual interest to your garden and to extend the spirea's blooming period throughout the spring.

Spiraea thunbergii is the earliest spirea to bloom. It is a twiggy shrub that grows to 5 feet tall with slender arching branches, feathery bright green leaves and small pure white flowers.

S. prunifolia 'Plena,' also known as bridalwreath, often finds its way from the garden into a bridal bouquet and wedding decorations. It grows up to 6 feet tall with slender, upright branches and shiny dark green leaves. The double flowers are long-lasting.

The large, showy *S.* x *vanhouttei*, which grows 6 to 8 feet high with gracefully arching branches, is the most commonly cultivated spirea. The pure white flowers are in clusters 1 to 2 inches wide.

S. veitchii grows up to 12 feet high with spreading, arching branches.

Spireas grow best in rich, moist loam, but will grow in most soils. They prefer a sunny location. Most are hardy from Zone 4 to 9.

The bright white flowers of Korean stewartia, **top,** *grow on a small tree.* **Right:** *Calla lilies.*

KOREAN STEWARTIA— STEWARTIA KOREANA

STEWARTIA is a small tree whose big white flowers and unusual bark will endear it to evening gardeners. In late summer, 3-inch white flowers that resemble single white roses bloom abundantly. When accented with lighting, the attractive mottled, flaking bark makes the tree remarkable even when not in bloom.

Korean stewartia is a handsome tree that can grow to 20 feet tall. In autumn, the leaves turn a lovely purplish-red. It thrives in sandy loam that has been enriched with peat moss or compost and grows best in partial shade. It is hardy to Zone 6.

CALLA LILY— ZANTEDESCHIA AETHIOPICA

AT NIGHT, atop almost invisible green stems, calla lily flowers remind me of elegant white

Art Nouveau vases. There is a beauty and grace to these flowers that is unmatched by anything else in the evening garden. Look closely at the flower and you will see how it appears iridescent. Even the leaves, seen during the day, are elegant with their large arrowhead shape, growing 1 to 3 feet tall.

I saw calla lilies in one evening garden where the leaves got more play than the flowers. An enlarged shadow cast on a white wall, created by a spotlight aimed through the leaves toward a wall, was a dramatic focal point in the garden.

Calla lilies are summer-flowering bulbs. In areas north of Zone 7, dig up the rhizome each fall and store it in a cool dark place in peat moss. Although I live in Zone 6, I have had great luck with calla lilies. Two have come back each year for seven or eight years without digging them up in the fall. I grow them in a sheltered area, almost against the south-facing side of the house. This microclimate is perfect for many nonhardy bulbs.

In cool areas, start the plant indoors in a pot in early spring. The soil should be kept constantly moist once the plant is in leaf. Plant it in full sun outdoors after the danger of frost has passed. After it has flowered, feed it once a week with liquid fertilizer. Cut back on watering in midsummer. Calla lilies are hardy to Zone 7.

As light diminishes in the evening and other flowers begin to fade, white calla lilies appear to glow, almost as if lit from within.

Night Bloomers

The flowers of brugmansia, **above and opposite,** *open in the evening.*

Aʟʟ ᴛʜᴇ ғʟᴏᴡᴇʀs in this select group are for the exclusive enjoyment of those who rise to the challenge of creating a garden for evening enjoyment. They are out of the domain of the common day gardener because they bloom only at night.

All the other plants that I recommend in this book for the evening garden can be planted in a daytime garden and still be enjoyed. However, night-blooming flowers in a day garden do not have the same

impact as at night. These plants should be honored in the evening garden with a special location—one that shows their full splendor and that allows a clear view of any nocturnal pollinators.

Many of the night-blooming plants are best suited to warm climates. However, they can be grown by northern gardeners in a greenhouse or with grow lights and then moved outside for summer enjoyment.

My day garden is designed for a faster pace than my evening garden.

Although I try to sit and enjoy the garden for half an hour at midday, before I know it, I've spotted something that needs picking, pruning or weeding. Sunlight is the great illuminator, showing off faults all too well. In an evening garden, the dimmer light forces me to slow down—the weeds and overgrown plants become invisible.

Like most people, I live a stressful life, and anything that encourages me to relax is great. Admittedly, there are many nights when I don't

go out into the garden, but when I do, I must take my time. It takes a while just for my eyes to adjust to the dimmer light. The large-flowered night-blooming plants grab my attention—I watch them as they open their flowers wide, inviting pollinators to drink their nectar.

For years, I was content with moonflowers. Any summer evening I could go outside at dusk and watch as they performed their nightly ballet. From a tight bud, they seemed to slowly twirl until the flower was completely open. After a while, I became jaded and began to take my moonflowers' waltz for granted.

I then had the honor to view the dance of several other night bloomers. The night-blooming cacti add a measure of suspense—which

Cactus flowers, such as those of saguaro, attract nocturnal pollinators.

night of the year will the flowers grace us with their presence?

The first time I watched a cereus open (and in all honesty, every time since), I was in awe. Gradually the swollen bud opened, layer by layer. Each layer that was revealed seemed more beautiful and delicate than the one before. Sometimes there was a pause in the sensual unveiling, and I wondered if it was to end there. But more and more petals were revealed, more, it seemed, than could have possibly fit into what was just a mere bud a short while ago.

At last, the flower was completely open. Some of the outer petals curled back and even the inner petals flared, revealing, almost brazenly, the sex organs of the flower—the pistil and stamens. We are quick to forget that these beautiful spectacles are frantic dances for survival.

A good clue to the type of pollinator of a night-blooming plant is the substance of the flower. Flowers that look delicate are usually pollinated by moths. Those with more sturdy flowers, like the saguaro, can withstand a bat's face literally rubbing into their petals.

ANGEL'S TRUMPET— BRUGMANSIA 'CHARLES GRIMALDI'

DURING THE DAY, the long yellow-orange flowers of this angel's trumpet just hang on the plant; they are attractive but not showstoppers. Once the sun goes down, the trumpets seem to come to life. They swell and stand out slightly from the

branches. At this time, they release their haunting perfume. 'Charles Grimaldi' is in his element at night.

Angel's trumpet is the common name given to both datura and brugmansia. There has been some debate as to which plants are datura and which are brugmansia. In general, brugmansia's trumpets hang down, while datura's point outward. Brugmansias are most often treated as tender perennial shrubs, while daturas are treated as annuals.

Brugmansias, native to South America, often look like small trees. The large trumpet-shaped flowers range from 6 to 20 inches long. All except *B. sanguinea* are very fragrant in the evening. The plants themselves have a semiupright habit, but the branches tend to bend, presenting a graceful appearance.

'Betty Marshall' is an interesting cultivar with spicy, sweet white flowers on a compact plant. *B. suaveolens* is an impressive 7- to 10-foot-high tree with long velvety green leaves and white flowers.

Brugmansia thrives outdoors during the summer, but before the first frost, bring it inside. Force the plant into dormancy—trim the foliage, cut back on watering and store it in a cool dark cellar or garage until spring. Be sure the temperature does not go below freezing. In spring, bring it into the light and start watering. Feed with 20-20-20 every two or three weeks from spring to fall.

Brugmansias are best grown as container plants in well-drained potting soil in full sun. They are hardy in Zones 9 and 10.

SAGUARO—
CARNEGIEA GIGANTEA

THE SAGUARO IS the stately cactus whose humanlike profile is a symbol of the desert of the American Southwest. In May, the flower buds make the tops of the arms look fingered.

At night, the waxy flowers open like flattened upturned trumpets, beckoning to the bats that fly up from Mexico to feast on the nectar and pollen. These bats do not home in on the cactus with their radar. Instead, the white flowers are so visible in the desert sky that they act like white flags summoning the bats to them. Bats bury their faces in the flowers—their long tongues are perfect for sucking out the nectar and then licking off any pollen that has stuck to their bodies.

This large night-blooming cactus is native to parts of Mexico, Arizona and California. Its habit is columnar and branching, although it is so slow growing that it may take 30 or more years before the first branch appears. Eventually, it can reach a height of 50 feet. It has prominent ribs that give it a fluted appearance. The ½- to 3-inch spines are light brown.

I have seen saguaro growing in cool greenhouses in the Far North. In the Southwest, it is perfectly happy outdoors, but cannot withstand temperatures below freezing for more than 24 hours.

Saguaro grows in full sun in well-drained soil. A word of caution—the flowers, though pretty, have the am-

Fragrant night-flowering jessamine.

monia odor of rotting fruit that attracts bats, so you would not want a saguaro next to your bedroom window. It is hardy in dry regions of the Southwest.

OLD MAN CACTUS—
CEPHALOCEREUS SENILIS

IN APRIL, 2-inch-long rose-colored flowers open in the evening above the thatch of long grayish-white hair that give this cactus its name. It is very adaptable and can be grown as an indoor potted plant in a cold climate. This cactus has a slender columnar habit. The 1½-inch-long spines are yellow and partly visible beneath the hair. Although it can reach 40 feet high, it is usually seen at half that height or less since it is very slow growing.

Water newly planted cacti sparingly to avoid rotting the dormant roots. Once the roots are active, within four to six weeks, water thoroughly. Allow the soil to dry before watering again. In the fall, cut back on water to allow the plants to go

dormant. Feed monthly in spring and summer.

Old man cactus needs full sun and well-drained soil. It is hardy in the Southwest.

NIGHT-FLOWERING
JESSAMINE—
CESTRUM NOCTURNUM

I DISCOVERED BY ACCIDENT that the release of fragrance by jessamine flowers seems to be triggered by the absence of light, rather than the time of day. When I brought home my first plant, it was in full flower. I put it in the dining room and did not turn off the lights until nearly midnight. Until then, the jessamine was nearly odorless. I awoke at 2 A.M. to discover that the scent had permeated the house. The next night, I did not turn on any lights in the dining room, and the fragrance was evident within a half hour after sunset.

Night-flowering jessamine is a slender-branched shrub native to the West Indies that can grow to 12 feet tall. The oblong leaves are evergreen and may reach 8 inches in length. The ¾-inch greenish-white to cream-colored flowers are tubular with erect or spreading petals. It usually blooms in winter or spring. Some people find the scent too strong—much like that of paperwhite narcissus.

In most areas, it is best grown as a container plant as it cannot tolerate night temperatures in winter below 50 degrees F. After the plant blooms, allow it to go partially dormant by

Some daylilies, **above and opposite**, *actually open in the late afternoon and stay in bloom through the night.*

keeping the soil fairly dry for about six weeks. Following this, prune the plant back hard and repot it in fertile, porous soil. Water well and allow it to flourish for another season.

Grow night-flowering jessamine in full sun to partial shade in ordinary garden soil. It is hardy in Zone 10.

EPIPHYLLUM OXYPETALUM

THERE ISN'T ONE epiphyllum I don't like for its showy flowers. Who among us does not enjoy the beauty of a Christmas or orchid cactus? But the most exciting by far is *Epiphyllum oxypetalum*. One night a year, its impressive white and buff flowers open to reveal their splendor. It is related to and has been con-

fused by some home growers with *Hylocereus undatus*. Epiphyllum has the advantage that it blooms at a younger age and can be kept within bounds by pruning.

Epiphyllum is relatively easy to grow indoors. Plant it in light, well-drained soil and keep it in bright light. Avoid direct sun, which scorches the leaves. Once the buds are set, do not move the plant or you will risk the buds dropping off. It is hardy in Zone 10.

DAYLILY— HEMEROCALLIS SP.

DOES A night-blooming daylily sound like an oxymoron? There are a number of daylilies that

open after 4 P.M., stay open all night and then close in the late morning. Beware, some daylilies are nocturnal in warm climates but diurnal, or day-flowering, in cooler areas.

Still other daylilies are known as extended bloomers—they stay open for 16 hours or more. Diurnal extended bloomers may open in the early morning but stay open until midnight, rather than closing early in the night like the typical diurnal daylily.

The daylily is not a true lily, but it is in the same botanical family. The name describes the flower perfectly. Each flower lasts only one day. On an individual daylily plant, there may be several flower scapes, each with the potential for a dozen or more successive buds. This assures that flowering will occur over an extended period of time.

The range of plant size is great—grassy-leaved miniatures grow only 6 to 10 inches high, while sturdy straplike-leaved plants grow 3 or more feet tall.

The flowers also vary in size, form and color. Flowers range from flat to trumpet-shaped and star-shaped to round. Petals may be recurved or ruffled. Some daylilies have double flowers with more than 12 segments.

Many years of hybridizing have created daylilies of nearly every color of the rainbow, with only true blue and pure white still to be achieved. In nature, however, daylilies are limited to shades of yellow, orange and a color referred to as fulvous—a blend of orange, yellow and red as seen in the ubiquitous *H. fulva*, the daylily species that grows along roadsides and is often incorrectly called tiger lily.

Daylilies are fibrous-rooted, hardy herbaceous perennials, not tubers, bulbs or rhizomes. Emerging in early spring, the long, narrow, heavily ribbed leaves form a fan.

When planning your garden, choose varieties to extend the season of bloom. The first flowers may appear in March in the Deep South and California, although the same variety may not bloom until May or June in northern areas. Flowering continues until fall in the North, but usually ends by late summer in warmer areas.

When you purchase daylilies by mail or at a local nursery, check to see if the variety is diurnal, nocturnal or an extended bloomer of either type. Some of my recommendations for diversity in an evening garden include the following:

'Pat Mercer' is a nocturnal extended bloomer with an interesting trait—the flowers open in the evening, displaying red petals and a green throat throughout the night and into the following morning. By late morning, the flower becomes more orange and the throat color

changes to white. This is indeed an exceptional daylily. None of the other recommended varieties have such chameleonlike qualities.

'After the Fall' is an extra-early-blooming daylily with 2¼-inch-diameter flowers. It is a fragrant nocturnal daylily with extended bloom.

'Beauty to Behold' blooms midseason with large 5½-inch-diameter light lemon flowers with ruffled edges.

'Bitsy' is a delightfully small nocturnal plant, growing only 20 inches high, that blooms extra early and continues well into the summer. It

has small 2-inch-diameter yellow trumpet-shaped flowers with slightly ruffled petals.

'Blossom Valley' is an 18-inch-high midseason nocturnal daylily with unusual coloration. The large 6½-inch-diameter flowers are light orchid-pink with a gold throat and ruffled edges.

'Border Giant' is a midseason nocturnal daylily that will often flower again later in the season if the stem is cut down after the plant stops blooming. Only 16 inches tall, the plants bear 7-inch frosty melon-pink blossoms with orchid ribs.

'Chorus Line' is an early diurnal daylily with extended bloom that grows to 20 inches high. The fragrant 3½-inch-diameter flowers are a stunning pink with a rose band above a yellow halo and a dark green throat.

'Cosmic Hummingbird' is the perfect name for this nocturnal, fragrant, extra-early-blooming plant. The 3½-inch-diameter flowers are peach with ruby-red eyes and stay open well into the morning. The plant is 26 inches tall.

'Diamond Anniversary' is an exceptionally vigorous nocturnal daylily that grows 32 inches high. It blooms in early midseason and will rebloom later in the summer if all the flowering stems are removed before it sets seed. The 6½-inch-diameter flowers are velvety with rounded petals of soft peach-pink blends.

'Evening Bell' has magnificent 7-inch-diameter yellow flowers with greenish-yellow throats. A nocturnal daylily with extended bloom, it grows to 22 inches tall.

'Gloria Blanca' is about as close to white as a daylily gets. The 6-inch-diameter near-white flowers with green throats are diurnal with blooms that last to midnight. It flowers in midseason and grows to 22 inches high.

'Hudson Valley,' with its magnificent 8-inch-diameter light yellow flowers with green throats, opens at night and lasts throughout the next day. A midseason daylily, it is prominent in the garden, growing to 32

When fully opened, the flower of Hylocereus undatus, below and opposite, measures 12 inches across.

inches high.

'Paul Bunyan' is a stalwart night-blooming daylily. The plants grow up to 40 inches tall, blooming in midseason with light gold ruffled flowers. They shimmer so much in the evening garden that they seem to be dusted with diamonds. Cut off the flowering stems before they set seed and this giant will likely rebloom.

Daylilies are readily available from numerous sources—mail-order plant catalogs, specialty breeders, and local nurseries and garden centers. The easiest, least expensive way to obtain plants is from people who are already growing daylilies. A single daylily plant can, if grown in ideal soil and

conditions, be left for 10 to 15 years. Eventually, however, it needs to be divided in order to rejuvenate the plant. See what your friends, neighbors and relatives are growing. People are usually more than happy to share their plants.

Plant daylilies almost anytime from spring through fall. Avoid planting them in extreme heat (over 90 degrees F) as their chances of rotting will be increased. Mail-order plants need to be soaked for several hours in tepid water before planting. Space daylilies 18 to 24 inches apart. The crown (the area where the roots and leaves join) should be no more than 1 inch below the soil. Once es-

tablished, fertilize the plants with a general-purpose organic fertilizer once in early spring and again in the fall after blooming.

Daylilies are easy to grow. They prefer at least six hours of sun a day. The paler colors benefit from full sun, while darker colors can tolerate partial shade. Although daylilies will grow in almost any type of soil, a slightly acidic rich loam with good drainage is ideal. They are hardy to to Zone 4.

NIGHT-BLOOMING CEREUS—
HYLOCEREUS UNDATUS

THE BLOOM OF this cactus is cause for celebration and a great excuse for a party. In summer, keep an eye on the plant. You will at some point notice flower buds forming. The buds will grow to about 12 inches in length before you have to start planning a cereus party.

When the buds become erect and look like they are ready to pop, call all your friends. Tell them to arrive at about 9 P.M. At that time, the tantalizing show will begin.

Slowly, the buds unwrap, one petal at a time. The fully opened flower is impressive, spanning 12 inches across. The narrow creamy-yellow outer petals are recurved as if to better show off the layers of broad pure white inner petals. The inner petals surround the prominent creamy-yellow stamens like a hoop-petticoat. All this plus a musty scent intended to attract the bats that pollinate this magnificent flower in its native Brazil.

Regale and enjoy the splendor of the flowers that remain strong and firm until daybreak. At that point, they collapse like a deflated balloon. That's it—the party's over until next year.

This cactus, which is related to cereus, is not for every household. If you have that special, bright, out-of-the-way place, it will reward you one night a year with its magnificent blooms.

Hylocereus has thick succulent stems with three prominent ribs. It climbs by aerial roots that dangle from the stem.

All cereus relatives (*Hylocereus, Lemaireocereus, Monvillea, Nyctocereus* and *Selenicereus*) grow best in soil that is coarse and fertile with ample sand or vermiculite so that it is completely free-draining. They like to be pot-bound. Allow the lower portion of the stem and the top of the uppermost roots to show at the surface of the soil. When the plant is young, repot it every two to three years. As it gets older and moves into a 10-inch or larger pot, it can wait longer between repottings.

Grow on a sunny window in a cool room from fall to spring. In summer, it can be placed in a partially shaded spot outdoors. Soak the soil thoroughly. Let it dry almost completely before resoaking. In summer, water about once a week. In winter, there

should be longer intervals between waterings. If pot-bound, fertilize with liquid houseplant fertilizer monthly from spring to early fall. Stems tend to be weak or trailing and may need support. It is hardy in Zone 10.

ORGAN-PIPE CACTUS—
LEMAIREOCEREUS THURBERI

AN ORGAN-PIPE cactus is a wonderful addition to a western evening garden for its shape alone. Anyone who has seen an organ-pipe cactus knows how it comes by its name: It is a columnar treelike cactus that branches from the base, resembling its namesake. Only if it is injured will it branch from the top.

The gray-green to dark green stems have 12 to 17 prominent ribs. The black spines are ½ to 1 inch in length. It is a slow-growing plant that eventually reaches a height of 15 feet.

In May or June, 3-inch-diameter purplish flowers with white edges make their annual nocturnal appearance. The pollinated flowers give rise later in the season to 1½-inch-long red-green fruit.

Organ-pipe cactus grows in full sun. It needs soil with excellent

Nyctocereus has a climbing habit.

drainage. Like all cacti, it requires little watering and is excellent for drought-tolerant gardens. It is hardy in the Southwest.

MONVILLEA—
MONVILLEA SP.

MONVILLEAS are night-blooming relatives of the cereus, native to the South American deserts. They are wild-looking in their native habitat, forming thickets with their sprawling slender stems. However, they can be contained and allowed to clamber around a sunny, warm greenhouse.

The flowers develop near the terminal ends of the stems. The outer petals of the flowers are generally pinkish to greenish and the insides are white or yellow. Both the stamens and styles are white. The withered flower does not fall off the plant, which gives it a rather untidy look.

Species of interest include the following:

M. cavendishii grows from 3 to 10 feet tall, branching from the base. Its stems are about 1 inch thick with 9 or 10 ribs. The needlelike spines are in clusters of 8 or 12, spaced less than ½ inch apart. The white flowers are somewhat funnel-shaped, about 4 to 5 inches in length, with petals that spread to about the same width at the end.

M. phatnosperma, native to Paraguay, sends up 3- to 6-foot bright green stems that are 1 inch thick with four to five ribs. The white flowers are 5 inches long.

M. spegazzinii, native to Argentina and Paraguay, has an erect habit. It has unusual white-spotted, bluish-green, three-ribbed stems. Young branches have dark spines with broadly conical bases grouped in threes. Mature branches, have one central spine surrounded by five radial spines. The 4½- to 5-inch-long funnel-shaped flowers are off-white inside and purplish outside.

As with other cacti, monvilleas can be grown outside in frost-free areas or in a greenhouse in colder climates. They require coarse fertile soil that is well drained. Amend soil with sand or vermiculite. Repot monvilleas every two to three years until they are in 10-inch or larger pots, then they can wait longer between repottings.

Grow in a sunny window in a cool room from fall to spring. In summer, move them to a partially shaded spot outdoors and water about once a week. In winter, there should be longer intervals between waterings. They are hardy in Zone 10.

NIGHT-BLOOMING CEREUS—
NYCTOCEREUS SP.

NYCTOCEREUS is yet another genus of cacti with the common name night-blooming cereus. This is why it is so important to refer to plants by their botanical names. Botanical names are universal, common names may differ from region to region. Very often, as is the case with night-blooming cereus, more than one plant may have the same common name.

In general, nyctocereus has a trailing or clambering habit. The stems are thin, ribbed and very spiny. The flowers, with relatively long calyx tubes with small scales and tufts of woolly hair and bristling spines, are white and funnel-shaped and open only at night. Some of the most commonly grown species include the following:

N. guatemalensis, native to Guatemala, has a fairly upright habit with arching or creeping stems 2½ inches thick. The spines are clustered with about 10 radial spines and three to six central spines up to 1¼ inches long. The fragrant 7-inch-long flowers are white inside and yellow to reddish-brown outside.

N. hirschtianus, native to Nicaragua, has narrow prostrate or pendulous stems with 10 ribs. The 2-inch-long narrow-petaled flowers are white to pinkish.

N. serpentinus (*Cereus serpentinus*) has a pendulous or creeping habit. The cylindrical 10 to 13 ribbed stems grow to 10 feet long with a 1- to 2-inch diameter. Flowers develop at or near the tip of the stems. The flowers are about 3½ inches wide and 6 to 8 inches in length with long bristly spines.

In warm regions without frost, grow nyctocereus outdoors, allowing it to sprawl. It also may be trained on supports. In all other areas, grow it in a greenhouse in the same manner as monvillea. It is hardy in Zone 10.

FOUR O'CLOCK (MARVEL OF PERU)— MIRABILIS JALAPA

THE COMMON NAME of this lovely annual comes from the time of day that the flowers open— the late afternoon. It is not the fading light, per se, that triggers these flowers to open, it is the concurrent fall in temperature. Once even one flower has opened, the event is heralded by a rich fragrance released into the surrounding air. The flowers close the next morning, except on dull, cloudy days.

This freely branching plant has an erect habit and an abundance of 2- to 6-inch-long heart-shaped leaves. Showy 1- to 2-inch yellow, white,

Four o'clocks, **below,** *are a fragrant annual named for the time of day when the flowers open.*

red or striped trumpet-shaped flowers are produced in profusion throughout the summer. Hybrid varieties include a dwarf four o'clock and one with variegated foliage.

In warm areas, sow the seeds directly in the garden in spring. In other areas, start the seeds indoors about eight weeks before the final frost date in spring. Transplant the seedlings into the garden at the same time you would set out tomatoes. Allow 12 inches between plants.

Four o'clocks thrive in ordinary garden soil in full sun or partial shade. Even in the coldest parts of the country, you may be rewarded with numerous volunteer seedlings in subsequent years.

EVENING PRIMROSE— OENOTHERA SP.

IF YOU HAVE BEEN reading this section and are beginning to lament about the paucity of night-

blooming plant material suitable for temperate gardens, here are some wonderful plants for your evening garden. There are over 80 species of evening primrose, many of which are

prized for their nocturnal flowers.

One word of caution, although all the *Oenothera* can be grouped together and are commonly called evening primrose, be sure of the species before you plant it. Do not make the same mistake I did, edging one of my early evening gardens with what I was told was evening primrose only to find that it was *O. biennis* or *O. fruticosa*, both more commonly known as sundrop, which close their flowers at night. At least it had the decency to wait until it was completely dark, so it was still of value in the late afternoon and into sunset.

The best known of the evening primroses is *O. macrocarpa* (formerly known as *O. missourensis*), the Missouri primrose. When I was photographing at the Missouri Botanical Garden last summer, I was told to not even bother looking at the plant until 8:30 P.M., which was well after sunset. I found it growing in the rock garden outside the temperate greenhouse. Indeed, I wouldn't have looked twice at it during the day— it grows 12 to 24 inches tall with 4-inch-long slightly hairy leaves.

I photographed other areas of the garden and returned at 8:25 P.M. Promptly at 8:30 P.M., the buds began to pop open and soon the plant was nearly covered with enormous lemon-yellow flowers. One of the hardiest of evening primroses, Missouri primrose can grow from Zone 4 to 10.

Some other interesting varieties of evening primrose include the following:

O. acaulis (*O. taraxacifolia*), which is native to Chile, starts out stemless, but forms 6-inch prostrate stems as it gets older. The dandelionlike leaves are 4 to 8 inches long. The 2- to 3-inch-diameter flowers

are white upon first opening and fade to pink as they age.

O. argillicola is a perennial or biennial native to the southern Appalachian Mountains. In its first year, it forms stemless rosettes of 3- to 7-inch-long leaves. In its second year, it forms prostrate, leafy flowering stems, which grow 2 to 3 feet long. It produces bright yellow flowers 2½ to 4 inches wide and will grow in most any well-drained soil.

Some evening primroses, such as Oenothera speciosa, **opposite,** *make ideal night-blooming plants, while sundrops,* **above,** *are attractive until sunset, when the flowers close.*

O. caespitosa is a perennial or biennial native to Nebraska and South Dakota. It is nearly stemless with a cluster of hairy, dandelionlike leaves up to 12 inches long. The 1½- to 3-inch flowers may be white or pink, deepening in color as they age.

O. californica, a perennial native to the deserts of California and Baja, California, differentiates itself by having underground rhizomes. The leaves are variable in shape and size. The 1½- to 2¼-inch-diameter flowers, borne in clusters, are white and fade to pink as they mature.

O. erythrosepala, a biennial possibly of garden origin, has naturalized in much of North America. It has basal rosettes of large leaves. In its second year, it develops 3- to 4-foot red-warted stems with crinkled leaves. The 2½ to 3½-inch-diameter flowers are yellow.

Any of the evening primroses make lovely additions to a sunny flower garden. Some are best suited to rock gardens or native plant gardens, while others are happy mixed in a perennial or annual border.

Evening primroses are very easy to grow. They grow readily from seed or, in the case of the perennial varieties, from cuttings. Sow seeds of annual varieties in early spring directly in the garden in well-drained sandy soil or loam. Thin seedlings, allowing 3 to 4 inches between plants. Most are hardy to Zone 5.

NIGHT-BLOOMING CEREUS MOON CEREUS— SELENICEREUS

SELENICEREUS IS yet another of the cereus relatives that is commonly called a night-blooming cereus. The genus name is derived from the Greek *selene*, or moon, referring to its nocturnal flowering habit.

Selenicereus are climbing or trailing cacti with long, slender ribbed stems. In the wild, they are epiphytic—they may be found growing on trees and sometimes hanging from cliffs. Some species have clusters of spines, bristles or hairs, while others are smooth. The large sweetly-scented flowers are usually white.

Selenicereus grandiflorus, **left and opposite,** *are climbing or trailing cacti that grow readily, even in containers, if given adequate support.*

The most commonly cultivated species is *S. pteranthus*. It has bluish-green stems ½ inch in diameter. Occasionally, the stems are tinged with purple. The tiny black spines are single or in clusters of up to four spines.

The flowers are very fragrant and may grow up to 12 inches long. The inside is white with reddish to bronzy yellow or purplish outside.

There are several other selenicereus worth mentioning:

S. boeckmannii has ¾-inch-wide stems that are sharply angled with eight or fewer ribs. The 15-inch-long flowers are white inside and brownish outside.

S. donkelaarii has stems that are only ½ inch wide, yet grow to 25 feet in length with 9 or 10 ribs. Spines are in clusters of 10 to 15. The 7-inch-long flowers are white on the inside, gradually fading to reddish on the outside.

S. grandiflorus has 1-inch-thick stems with fewer than nine ribs. The stems have clusters of needlelike spines mixed with white hair. It

bears 7-inch-long flowers that are white on the inside and salmon-pink on the outside.

S. hondurensis has ½-inch-wide stems with 7 to 10 ribs. The ¼-inch-long spines are interspersed with white bristles or hair. The 8-inch-long flowers are white inside and yellow to brownish outside.

S. macdonaldiae has stems ½ inch wide. Its flowers are immense, growing to 1 foot or more in length. They are white on the inside and reddish or yellowish on the outside.

S. spinulosus has 1- to 2-inch-wide angled stems with four to six ribs. It often has numerous aerial roots. The small spines are clustered with two central and five or six radial spines. The 5-inch flowers are white or pinkish.

Selenicereus are relatively easy to grow if there is adequate support and space for their vining stems. The stems may be trained on trellises, wires or stakes. In warm climates, they can be allowed to wander outside, climbing trees or

crawling over rocks. In frost-free climates, these cacti can be grown outside. In other areas, they can be successfully grown in a greenhouse and sometimes on a windowsill in a pot during the cold spells and then gently moved outside in summer. For specific cultural information, see *Hylocereus undatus* (page 101). It is hardy in Zone 10.

NIGHT PHLOX— ZALUZIANSKYA CAPENSIS (NYCTERINIA CAPENSIS)

I ONCE VISITED a moon garden that was planted with, among other plants, night phlox. Assertive but not overpowering in the night air, the perfume of the night phlox drew me toward the plant. The person who had created the garden was very clever—the night phlox was the only fragrant plant. Any other fragrance would have clashed with it or changed the scent, making it too pervasive.

The flowers of zaluzianskya resemble those of true phlox; however the two plants are not related. The ½-inch-diameter flowers are white marked with maroon and borne on umbrellalike clusters. Night phlox is an erect bushy annual that grows 9 to 18 inches tall. The margins and midribs of the leaves are fringed with hair.

Start the seeds indoors eight weeks before the last frost date. Transplant them into well-drained loam in the garden after all danger of frost has passed. Allow 12 inches between plants.

Silver Foliage

A half-hardy perennial, dusty miller glimmers in the moonlight.

SILVERY PLANTS brighten whatever space they occupy. At night, they glimmer in the moonlight. Look closely at a plant with silver or gray foliage. The leaves are not silver—they are actually green. Most have a silvery coating that gives this effect, others have fine white hairs that cover the leaves.

It may seem like one of Mother Nature's illusions, but there is a reason for the silvery coating. All of these drought-tolerant plants grow in arid climates with lots of sun. The silvery coating reflects the sunlight and keeps the leaves from scorching. It also helps cut down on moisture loss from leaf transpiration.

Because of their coating, most silvery plants do not tolerate much winter moisture. They demand full sun and well-drained soil. Most flourish in poor sandy soil. In wet soil, or when exposed to consistent high humidity and rain, they tend to rot. Many of the plants are grown for their foliage—their flowers are often insignificant.

SILVER MOUND ARTEMISIA— ARTEMISIA SCHMIDTIANA 'SILVER MOUND'

THIS IS A PLANT I feel compelled to touch whenever I am in my garden. It is a handsome perennial with soft silky leaves. It grows only 4 to 6 inches tall and spreads out to form a gently rounded mound. The small white or yellow flowers are not very showy. It is a perfect choice for a rock garden at night as it glows in the moonlight.

As the plant gets older, it has a tendency to flop open in the center. Pruning the foliage back before flowering can delay this.

Grow silver mound in full sun in sandy, well-drained soil. It is hardy to Zone 4.

CARDOON— CYNARA CARDUNCULUS

CARDOON IS a striking plant—the tallest of the silver plants for the evening garden, it grows to 6 feet high. It resembles a thistle, with large, very deeply cut spiny leaves—grayish-green above, white and feltlike below. The 3-inch-diameter flower heads are purple. In warm climates, cardoon can be grown as a perennial and is dramatic in any garden in late summer through fall.

Cardoon needs a long, cool growing season to reach its optimum size. Start seeds indoors in late winter. Transplant twice to successively larger pots before setting out into the garden. Allow at least 2 or 3 feet between plants.

Grow cardoon in rich soil in full sun. Keep evenly moist throughout the growing season. It is hardy in Zones 9 and 10.

LAVENDER—LAVANDULA SP.

LAVENDER IS an ideal plant for a large rock garden or a flower border in an evening garden. Plant it near a path so that when you pass by, you can gently brush the foliage and release the scent into the air. The silvery foliage is beautiful at sunset and in the moonlight.

Lavender is native to the Mediterranean mountains and coast. It is a shrubby multibranched plant with woody branches and narrow leaves. The fragrant flowers appear on the ends of long spikes.

Lavandula vera (English or true

The tallest of the silver-leaved plants, cardoon is both an unusual vegetable and a worthwhile addition the the evening garden.

lavender) is also known as *L. officinalis*, *L. angustifolia* and *L. spica*. It is a hardier perennial than French lavender (*L. stoechas*).

English lavender has blunt, narrow grayish-green leaves. In warm climates, it can grow to 3 feet tall or more. The small lavender flowers are grouped in whorls of 6 to 10.

French lavender has long, narrow grayish-green leaves. Its flowers are a rich dark purple. It is smaller, growing to about 12 inches high, and thrives in warm climates.

The easiest way to grow lavender is to purchase a young plant from a nursery in the spring. Set it out in the garden after all danger of frost has passed, allowing at least 12 to 18 inches between plants. In the first year, cut off any flowering stems as they appear. This treatment may seem severe, but in the long run you will have a healthier, more vigorous plant.

Lavender often begins to look ratty after about four years. The simplest solution is to replace it or cut it back severely to allow fresh new growth to emerge.

Lavender prefers a sunny location and light, dry, well-drained soil. Mulch the plant well in late autumn to protect it through the winter. Space permitting, the plant can be moved indoors for the winter and grown on a sunny windowsill or under lights. Lavender is hardy to Zone 6.

RUSSIAN SAGE (AZURE SAGE)— PEROVSKIA ATRIPLICIFOLIA

RUSSIAN SAGE is a shrubby perennial that grows 3 to 5 feet tall. The narrow silvery-white stems and small leaves covered with gray-white hairs give it an open airy look. In mid to late summer, small ¼-inch purplish-blue flowers are borne in scattered whorls along the stems and in spikes at the tips of the branches.

Russian sage needs the contrast of a dark background to be appreciated in the daytime. At night, however, it is luminous on its own. Plant it near a walkway where you can brush the foliage to release a mild sage aroma.

Russian sage thrives in full sun and well-drained soil. Although it will grow in shade, it has a tendency to sprawl. Each spring, cut the plant to the ground. This promotes stronger stems and more prolific flowering. It is hardy in Zones 5 and 6.

SAGE—SALVIA OFFICINALIS

SAGE'S GRAY-GREEN leaves do not have quite the lucent quality of some of the other gray-silver foliage

Tall, silvery Russian sage grows beside English lavender, left. **Opposite:** *Lavender cotton behind a planting of lavender.*

plants, but I include it in the garden for the wonderful aroma it emits when gently brushed. The blue flowers, which appear from late spring through early summer, add their own color when the late-afternoon sun sets them aglow.

The old Latin proverb *Cur moriatur homo, ciu salvia crescit in horto?* ("Why should a man die while sage grows in his garden?") pays homage to the high esteem in which sage has been held. Sage is an attractive perennial herb that grows 2 to 3 feet tall. The stems can become woody and gnarled as the plant gets older. The gray-green leaves are oblong in shape with a pebbled texture.

As well as the common culinary sage, I include several interesting cultivars in my edible-flower garden that are evening gems as well. 'Aurea' is a compact variety with yellow variegated leaves that is attractive in the garden but rarely flowers. The same is true for 'Tricolor,' whose lower leaves have white margins. Unfortunately, tricolor is not reliably hardy in winter.

Start sage seeds in spring or fall. Transplant them into the garden when the seedlings are 2 to 3 inches high and allow 12 to 18 inches between plants. Prune existing plants back by at least one third in spring to keep them bushy. Also prune back any dead wood at that time. Throw small pieces of pruned sage wood on the barbecue to add a unique smoked flavor to fish, pork and poultry.

Sage grows best in full sun or light shade. It prefers light, sandy, well-

drained soil that is evenly moist in summer, but dry in winter. In cold climates, lightly mulch sage in the fall with several inches of shredded leaves to protect it throughout the winter. It is hardy to Zone 3.

LAVENDER COTTON— SANTOLINA CHAMAECYPARISSUS (S. INCANA)

I FIRST SAW lavender cotton during the day in a marvelous planting at Filoli, a garden south of San Francisco. In St. Louis, I got to see it in the evening and it was outstanding. It was used in a formal herb gar-

den, and its lightness set off the entire garden. In Maryland, I saw it in bloom—its flowers towered above the plant. The silvery flower stalks caught my eye, magnificent from sunset through moonrise.

Lavender cotton is a silvery-gray evergreen perennial that grows from 1 to 2 feet tall. In northern gardens, it is often grown as an annual.

Lavender cotton demands full sun and well-drained soil. In areas where the temperature falls below freezing, mulch the plants well in the fall. It is easily propagated from stem cuttings that root in sand. In spring, prune the plants to keep a tidy, even form. It is hardy to Zone 6.

DUSTY MILLER—
SENECIO CINERARIA
(CENTAUREA MARITIMA,
CINERARIA MARITIMA)

IN MY LONG ISLAND garden, dusty miller has survived several winters. I have enjoyed its silvery foliage glinting in the moonlight for many seasons. It survived 18 inches of snow and ice that covered it for more than two weeks. When the snow melted, I gazed out in the evening, expecting to find flattened splotches of silver on the cold, wet soil. Instead, the perky plants were still upright and strong, showing themselves to full advantage in the light of the full moon.

Dusty miller is actually a half-hardy perennial, although it is commonly grown as an annual. Its leaves are thick and are covered with long white matted hairs. Some varieties have rounded leaves while others, 'Silver Dust' for example, have fern-like foliage. It ranges in height from 8 to 30 inches, depending on the variety.

If it overwinters successfully, dusty miller will bloom the second year. The flowers are yellow or cream, borne on small terminal clusters. Dusty miller is an excellent contrast in the garden when placed next to a plant with dark foliage. The gray color is also refreshing in the heat of the summer. During the day, it serves to cool down the hot reds and oranges of other annuals.

Start dusty miller seeds indoors 8 to 10 weeks before the last frost. Do not cover the seeds, as they need strong light and a temperature between 65 and 70 degrees F to germinate. Transplant dusty miller into the garden two to three weeks before the last frost. Allow 6 to 8 inches between plants.

Dusty miller thrives in warm weather planted in full sun and well-drained soil.

Silvery plants brighten whatever space they occupy. **Left:** *The Silver Garden at Longwood Gardens.*

Foliage for Contrast

Plants with vareigated leaves, such as caladium, come into their own after dark.

THE JOY OF plants with variegated leaves is that they show up in the evening, while their plain green-leaved cousins fade into the gloom. It is common to include variegated plants to brighten up the dark spots in a daytime garden. After dark, these plants really come into their own. All you perceive are the variegated areas, not the rest of the leaves, so these plants take on unusual forms.

As you look through seed catalogs and visit nurseries, you will notice that there are variegated varieties of many commonly grown plants. A red geranium with green leaves might be colorful in a window box during the day, but a red geranium with variegated leaves will be visible after dark.

Variegations are especially attractive for ground covers. Lilyturf (*Liriope*) is good as both a ground cover and an edging plant. Variegated lilyturf is outstanding in an evening garden with its light green colorations. Ivy (*Hedera* sp.) is one of the commonly grown ground covers for shady areas. Although attractive during the day, the green leaves are barely visible at night, unless you introduce one of the many variegated ivies ('Goldheart,' 'Glacier,' Gloire de Marengo, 'Adam,' 'Golden Snow,' 'Hazel,' 'Luzii' and 'Tricolor' are among the best).

When planting or replacing trees and shrubs, consider variegated choices. Many eastern gardeners are having to replace the native dog-

woods that are dying from disease.
Cornus contraversa 'Variegata,' with
its white-bordered leaves, is a perfect
substitute that is a focal point both
day and night.

Be careful not to overfertilize variegated plants as the extra nutrients
may turn some completely green.
Variegation is not a stable state, and
the tendency of most plants is to re-
vert to their natural color. If a variegated plant sends out a plain branch
or several nonvariegated leaves, cut
them off immediately.

VARIEGATED BISHOP'S WEED
(GOUTWEED)—
AEGOPODIUM PODAGRARIA
'VARIEGATUM'

A BED AND BREAKFAST I visited
on Vancouver Island, British
Columbia, had variegated bishop's
weed planted in beds along the path
that led from the parking area to the
house. It bordered the house, shar-
ing the beds with a variegated akebia
that climbed up the walls. Even in
dim light, the walkway was defined
as the dark area between the plantings of bishop's weed. The white
edging to the leaflets gave a luminous effect, visible even in the dim
light of the crescent moon.

Variegated bishop's weed is a hardy,
deciduous, shade-tolerant ground
cover. The ½- to 3-inch-long leaflets
form a dense mass. This plant is vig-

orous and may become invasive as it
spreads by underground rootstocks.
Keep it contained with an underground barrier of wood, metal, concrete or tough plastic. To keep the
plant low and uniform, mow it two
or three times a year Variegated
bishop's weed grows in any type of
soil. It is hardy to Zone 4.

VARIEGATED ITALIAN ARUM—
ARUM ITALICUM 'PICTUM'

T HIS TUBEROUS-ROOTED perennial is a striking addition to
the evening garden. Its narrow
spear-shaped leaves are boldly mar-

bled and veined in cream with a narrow green border.

This arum blooms in early summer. In bloom, it resembles a miniature cream-colored calla lily. In late
summer, spikes of red berries are displayed. The leaves emerge in late
summer or early fall, after the berry
spike has died back, and last through
the winter. After the plant flowers,
the leaves wither, leaving no evi-
dence of their existence.

It grows best in partial shade in a
humus-rich, moist soil. It is well
suited for a woodland garden or at
the edge of a shaded pond and is
hardy to Zone 5 or 6.

JAPANESE-PAINTED FERN— ATHYRIUM NIPPONICUM 'PICTUM' (A. GOERINGIANUM 'PICTUM')

Most ferns are interesting in an evening garden for their shape and architectural form. Japanese-painted ferns, however, are of more interest as a variegated plant.

The leaflets are purplish at the base, blending to lavender and continuing on to a silvery greenish-gray near the tips. Its horizontal, rather than vertical, growth habit displays its variegation pattern effectively. The fronds grow to 1½ feet long, forming a tight, slowly spreading clump. In mild areas, it remains evergreen; in more temperate locations, it is a deciduous perennial.

Japanese-painted ferns grow best in rich, damp soil in partial shade. After a frost, the fronds turn brown. Allow the fronds to remain on the plant to act as a protective mulch to shelter the growth that emerges in early spring. After the new fronds have come up, cut the old foliage back. They are hardy to Zone 5.

FLOWERING KALE, FLOWERING CABBAGE— BRASSICA OLERACEA: ACEPHALA GROUP

Flowering kale and flowering cabbage have become popular in the past decade as fall and winter annual bedding plants in northern gardens and as winter and early spring bedding plants in southern gardens. Their natural variegations

In fall and winter, ornamental kale and cabbage still provide visual interest.

add visual interest to the evening garden at a time when not much else can survive the punishing weather.

These showy plants are related to the edible brassicas. As a matter of fact, flowering kale is as tasty as any other kale. Flowering cabbage, however, is too tough and stringy to eat.

The plants have a short stem topped with a cluster of open leaves, more like a bibb lettuce than the typical tightly closed cabbage heads. Flowering kale is usually more frilly and delicate looking than flowering cabbage and has a more open growth habit. The leaves may have variegations of green with purple, cream, rose, pink or white.

Cold weather is not detrimental to flowering kales and cabbages. However, if the weather does not remain consistently cold, or there is a lot of rain or snow that melts on the

plants, get rid of them. Otherwise, the garden will take on the aroma of rotted cabbage.

Many nurseries now offer fully grown flowering cabbage and kale plants in the fall, but rarely in the spring. Unless you live in an area that has a long cool spring or is mild enough that you can plant them in winter, they last longer as a fall crop.

You have a greater choice of varieties if you grow the plants from seed. For fall plants, start the seeds in July in a cool semishaded area. In September, transplant them into the garden. Plant them in a sunny location or in partial shade in any type of well-drained soil.

FANCY-LEAVED CALADIUM— CALADIUM X HORTULANUM

WITH ITS LARGE fancy leaves in variegations of white, rose, salmon, red or green, caladium is a colorful and elegant addition to the summer evening garden.

I observed beds of different caladium at Park Seed in South Carolina last summer. As afternoon flowed into evening, the many shades of pink were suffused with the rosy colors of sunset. The leaves glowed for a brief moment. Finally, as dusk settled, the white portions remained visible. They had a cool look that betrayed the hot, humid evening.

Caladium is a showy foliage plant with large, elongated heart-shaped leaves that may be flat or ruffled and are always variegated. It can be planted outdoors or in containers for indoor enjoyment in winter. Depending on the variety used, it can subtly accent a dark spot in the garden or electrify a border at night.

There is a caladium for almost every taste:

'Candidum' has rather staid variegation—white leaves with prominent green veination and edges.

'White Queen' is a bit more striking, with white leaves shading to soft green at the edges and margined in deep green.

'Frieda Hemple' has almost electric red leaves with slightly paler veins, shading to green at the edges.

Caladium plants are grown from tubers. Start the tuber indoors at 70 to 80 degrees F. Plant it in a 3- to 4-inch pot in a mixture of one part potting soil and four parts humus, just deep enough to cover the tuber. Keep warm and well watered.

After the plant has developed three or four leaves, repot it. When the outside daytime temperature is consistently above 70 degrees F, the caladium can be transplanted into the garden. Allow 1 or 2 feet between plants. In warm climates, plant the tubers 1 inch deep and 12 inches apart in spring.

Enjoy the beauty of the caladium leaves throughout the summer. As the foliage begins to fade, cut back on watering. Before the first frost, dig up the tubers, permitting any soil attached to the roots to remain. Allow them to dry in a shady, airy spot

Caladium, **left**, *is an elegant addition to the summer evening garden.* **Opposite foreground:** *Gold hakonechloa shines in the autumn.*

for about a week. Remove any foliage and excess soil. For the winter, store the tubers between 50 and 60 degrees F in vermiculite or peat moss.

Caladium prefers rich, moist, well-drained soil. It is often thirsty and must never be allowed to go without water. It is hardy in Zones 9 and 10.

GOLD HAKONECHLOA— HAKONECHLOA MACRA AUREOLA

I WAS CHARMED the first time I saw this grass in a friend's Pennsylvania garden late one afternoon. Planted above a pond, it gave the illusion of a small, graceful waterfall. The yellow-green variegations caught the late afternoon light, their reflections glimmered in the pond.

When my friend came to visit me several months later, he gave me a small clump that I immediately planted in the north-facing bed by the swimming pool. It unifies that bed, and is also suggestive of the larger ornamental grasses at the east end of the pool. It softens the hard edge of the raised bed and is another delightful eye-catcher around the pool at night.

Gold hakonechloa is bright yellow-green and grows to about 2 feet when it is established. The foliage is soft and, unlike other grasses, falls to one side, resembling a lovely cascade of water.

Gold hakonechloa blooms in August and shimmers in the moonlit garden. Like other grasses, its sinuous movements in a breeze are entrancing. In autumn, the colors fade from the leaves and it becomes a wheat-beige color that lasts through the winter.

Gold hakonechloa prefers humusy, moist, rich, well-drained soil that is deeply cultivated. It grows best in light shade and is hardy to the southern limits of Zone 4 with winter protection.

YELLOW ARCHANGEL— LAMIASTRUM GALEOBDOLON

T HE SILVER SPOTS on the leaves of this shade-loving ground cover veritably glisten in the moonlight.

Lamiastrum is an attractive perennial with 1½-inch-long heart-shaped, toothed leaves that are spotted with silver. As a member of the mint family, it looks much like a variegated mint, and, like its relatives, it may be very invasive.

If you have a shaded area to brighten up, this plant will do it. In spring, ¾-inch yellow flowers appear in the dense clusters of the upper leaf axils. 'Herman's Pride' bears smaller metallic dark green leaves flecked with silver and grows to 8 inches tall. The cultivar 'Variegatum' has leaves that are mostly silver with green edges and veins.

Lamiastrum grows in full sun or shade in average soil. It is not a fussy plant. If you are concerned about its invasive habit, either plant it in a container or install metal or plastic barriers in the soil. It is hardy to Zone 4.

RIBBON GRASS (GARDENER'S GARTERS)—PHALARIS ARUNDINACEA PICTA

RIBBON GRASS made a lasting impression on me when I saw it at a Long Island estate. It was get- ting dark, and I had just finished photographing flowers in a charm- ing cutting garden. As I turned around, my attention was caught by something in the distance glimmer- ing in the dim light. I could not make out what it was, so I set off to inves-

The silver spots on yellow archangel, **opposite,** *a shade-loving ground cover, appear to glisten in the moonlight.* **Below:** *Ribbon grass thrives even in poor soil.*

Lungwort 'Mrs. Moon,' **left,** *a perennial ground cover that grows well in shady areas,* **right.**

tigate. As I approached, I realized that the wavering and shimmering was a planting of illuminated ribbon grass reflected in a small pond.

Ribbon grass, with its bold green and white striations, is a good choice for the evening garden, especially in an area with poor soil. It is semi-evergreen, growing about 3 feet high, and has the added benefit of retaining its color for most of the year. A word of caution, it spreads by underground rhizomes and can be invasive.

Ribbon grass grows in almost any type of soil, but drought, shade and clay soil will slow it down. It is hardy to Zone 4.

DWARF WHITESTRIPE BAMBOO— PLEIOBLASTUS VARIEGATUS

IF YOU LIKE the form of bamboo, but do not have a garden that can support a giant 20 feet or more in height, this bamboo is an excellent choice for your evening garden.

I once had the honor to be invited to the opening of a Japanese garden. I had a sneak preview the day before, but the garden was completely different at twilight. Many of the wonderful plantings and bamboo objects that had caught my eye in daylight were not so outstanding at twilight. What was impressive were the white stepping stones on the hillside, the white gravel path leading to a small icon and the grove of dwarf white-stripe bamboo.

This variegated bamboo has persistent leaves that maintain their distinctive green and white color throughout the winter. It grows to 3 feet tall with ¼-inch-diameter culms. Dwarf whitestripe bamboo is a running bamboo that needs a means of containment to keep it in place.

It grows in full sun or partial shade in well-drained soil. It is hardy to −10 degrees F.

LUNGWORT— PULMONARIA SP.

THE SILVERY SPOTS on the leaves of lungwort add interest to the evening garden in early spring. Lungworts are excellent perennial ground covers in shaded areas. Their basal leaves are somewhat hairy and range from 2 inches to over 1 foot long, depending on the variety.

Lungworts rarely grow more than 18 inches tall. They flower in early spring and are notoriously long bloomers. In a year with a mild winter, one bloomed in my garden from January to May.

The purplish-red or blue flowers are not very showy during the day, but they take on a special glow in the late afternoon and at sunset. Lungworts are an excellent backdrop for early spring-flowering bulbs.

Among the best choices for an evening garden are the following:

Pulmonaria officinalis 'Sissinghurst White' has 2- to 4-inch-long oval leaves spotted with silver and bears white flowers.

P. saccharata has broad 12-inch-long leaves, daintily dappled with silver and gray. Its flowers are rosy in bud and open to a violet blue.

P. saccharata 'Alba' has white flowers and leaves marbled with silver.

P. saccharata 'Mrs. Moon' is very popular as a ground cover for its handsome leaves with bright silver spots. The pink flowers fade to blue.

Lungworts grow best in cool, moist soil in partial to full shade. Divide plants in the fall, which is a good time to get one or two from a gardening friend. In spring, they are available at nurseries and through mail-order sources. Pulmonarias are hardy from Zone 3 to 9.

Fragrant Plants

Gardenia flowers provide a sweet tropical scent for the evening garden.

SCENT PLAYS A major role in my evening garden, especially in the summer. I enjoy walking around the property, catching the various aromas. Although some of the fragrances are subtle, I know where the plants are so I can seek them out and sniff their perfumes whenever I want.

In my rose garden, 'Mirandy' has a strong rose scent, while 'Tropicana' has a fruity overtone. 'Mr. Lincoln' has a robust smell, while 'Tiffany' is much more delicate. As I cross the lawn, the heady perfume of the tuberoses fills my nostrils. It is a strong, yet sensuous aroma.

Coming back toward my wing of the house, I anticipate the sweet fragrance of the moonflowers. I can smell them when I reach my parked car, yet I cannot see them around the corner of the house. The scent is stronger as they come into view. I can sit on the patio and look at them surrounding the windows—dozens upon dozens in bloom.

Continuing to the back of the house, flowering tobacco sweetens the air around the pool with its intoxicating perfume. I jump into the pool to cool off. Out of the pool, as I grab for my towel, I step on some of the lemon thyme planted in the gravel and between stepping stones. A rush of spicy lemon fills the air—adding to the sense of refreshment I feel from my swim. Walking back into the house, I pass by a small planting where I catch the country-fresh, sweet smell of mignonette.

When I stroll around a garden, I

admire the plants from a distance. What gets me up close is their fragrance. I reach up to grasp a lilac branch, and as I bring it closer to my face, I appreciate the shape and colors of the flowers more than if I had just casually walked past. As the song says, you have to stop to smell the roses. You can't appreciate scent on the run. In this harried world, it's good that plants force us to slacken our pace.

I was at Callaway Gardens in Georgia one New Year's. As I walked through the garden, admiring the lights in the trees, my nose caught a whiff of a sweet scent. I immediately gravitated toward the fragrance, which was somehow familiar, but also reminiscent of a different place and season. I was brought up short at the edge of a bed planted with paper-white narcissus. At home, I force them into bloom indoors for the holiday season. I had always found the fragrance overwhelming—too much for any small room. But outdoors, the perfume floated gently on the breeze and was not overpowering at all.

Some fragrances are temperature-related. Certain flowers may be wonderfully scented during the warmth of the day, but lose their aroma at night. Others, like tuberose and nicotiana, are fragrant only at night. Some scents seem to hover around the flower, while others fill the surroundings.

When planting fragrant flowers in a garden, be careful to space different varieties well. One scent may clash with another, and unfortunately, too much of a good thing—even wonderful fragrances—can destroy the mood.

One year, I had moonflowers, tuberoses and two varieties of nicotiana outside my bedroom window. On hot, windless nights, I had to close the window or risk olfactory overload.

I especially enjoy the reminiscences the evening garden evokes. The fragrance of a certain flower will often bring back long-forgotten memories. These scents are one more reason to relax and enjoy your evening garden and everything it brings to mind.

COFFEE—
COFFEA ARABICA

IF YOU THINK the aroma of freshly ground coffee beans is tantalizing, just wait until you have taken a whiff of the flowers of the coffee plant. Although only slightly fragrant during the day, after dark the flowers emit an evocative floral perfume that fills the room.

Coffee is a handsome upright foliage plant that grows to 15 feet tall. It has evenly spaced tiers of branches and dark, shiny, oval leaves up to 6 inches long.

In midsummer, ¾-inch flowers often form clusters near the leaf bases. The flowers last only a few days, followed by ½-inch fruits that start out green and turn purple or red when ripe. Within the fruit are two seeds—the coffee beans.

Place the coffee plant in a container with rich, well-drained potting soil. It prefers bright light, however direct sun will scorch the leaves. Move the plant outdoors in the summer to a shaded location.

To get the plant to flower, you need to keep it in an area with relatively high humidity. This may be difficult, especially in the winter when most homes are quite dry. If

Flowering tobaccos sweeten the night air with their intoxicating perfume.

Orange and lemon trees provide not only fruit but fragrance in the tropical garden. **Top:** *An orange tree.* **Bottom:** *Blossoms of the lemon tree.*

you can keep the humidity above 40 percent and the night temperatures in winter above 55 degrees F, you may be rewarded with flowers.

Try placing the container in a shallow tray filled about 2 inches deep with pebbles. Add water almost to the top of the pebbles. As the water evaporates, it will add moisture to the air around the tree.

Some growers suggest misting the plant with a water bottle, but this only gives short bursts of moisture that condense on the leaves and then evaporate. Consider adding a small humidifier to the room and placing it near the coffee plant. A humidifier increases the humidity to a comfortable 50 to 60 percent, without making the room feel like a steamy indoor jungle.

Even if your coffee plant doesn't bloom, you will still have a handsome foliage plant.

LEMON—CITRUS LIMON
ORANGE—CITRUS SINENSIS

IF YOU LIVE in a suitable climate, you should have a lemon or orange tree to perfume the evening garden. The star-shaped white flowers of both plants are delightful at night, and they have an intoxicating fragrance. The added bonus is the fruit that ripens months after the flowers (from October through June). There is almost nothing that can beat going outside and picking a fresh orange from your own tree for breakfast.

Lemons and oranges are handsome

Evening Gardens

landscape trees grown in warm areas. If you live in a colder climate, you need not be deprived of the beauty and fragrance of citrus, you just have to be content with a portable-size dwarf citrus that is well suited for growing in a container.

Lemon trees are small, ranging from 10 to 20 feet in height. They have an open growth habit and lightly thorned branches. The semiglossy green leaves are elliptical with crenated edges. The 1-inch star-shaped lemon flowers are very fragrant. They are white inside and streaked with violet outside.

Oranges are large, round, formal-looking trees that grow 20 to 35 feet tall. The trunk and branches are occasionally spined. The leaves, dark green above with yellow spots and light green below with dark green spots, are fragrant when crushed. The small, fragrant 1-inch white flowers appear singly or in small clusters from February to April.

When purchasing a tree, look for a cultivar suitable for your climate. Citrus can be planted at any time, but they do best when planted in the late winter or early spring. When planting, allow 20 to 35 feet around each tree.

Citrus need plenty of water until they are well established. Water every two to five days in hot, dry areas. In moist areas, watering every week or two may be sufficient. Mulch well around the tree, taking care not to mulch right up to the trunk. There are specific fertilizers for citrus. Apply as directed, but do not feed after midsummer.

Dwarf citrus adapt readily to container cultivation. In cooler climates, the plants can be grown outdoors during the warm months and taken indoors during the cool months. Indoors, they require bright light and cool days and nights—not over 65 degrees F for flower production. Do not allow the soil to become dry.

In general, citrus need full sun. They prefer light, well-drained, fertile, loamy soil rich in organic matter. Citrus are hardy to Zones 9 and 10.

GARDENIA (CAPE JASMINE)— GARDENIA JASMINOIDES

I AM ENVIOUS of gardeners who live in warm enough areas to grow gardenias outdoors. I once visited a garden in South Carolina where I was awestruck by a gardenia that was taller than I am. At night, the glossy leaves reflected some light, but it was the roselike flowers and their sweet tropical fragrance that stole the show.

Outdoors, gardenias are handsome evergreen shrubs with bright, glossy 3- to 4-inch-long leathery leaves and beautiful, extremely fragrant 2- to 3½-inch-wide white flowers. Under the right conditions, gardenias will bloom from spring through summer.

Northern gardeners can grow small houseplant versions of this lovely shrub. Even these plants, when moved outdoors, add a touch of the exotic to the summer evening garden.

There are a number of cultivars on the market, including the following varieties:

'August Beauty' grows 4 to 6 feet tall. It blooms from spring to fall with luscious, double flowers.

'Golden Magic' grows to 3 feet tall and is equally well suited for growing outdoors in the South or in a large container indoors in the North.

Under the right conditions, gardenias bloom from spring through summer.

Not to be confused with the common gladiolus, Gladiolus tristis, above, produces a sweet fragrance at night. Opposite: Kahili ginger can grow up to eight feet tall.

ture, perfect as a houseplant in the winter and small enough to be easily carried outdoors in summer. Its leaves are often variegated. Southerners can use it as a ground cover.

'Veitchii' is a common pot plant that grows 3 to 4 feet tall and blooms from spring to fall.

Plant gardenias high, as you would azaleas or rhododendrons, in a location where they will not be in competition with the roots of other plants. They are shallowly rooted, so do not cultivate around the plants.

Gardenias grow best in rich, acidic, moisture-retentive, well-drained soil. Amend the soil with organic matter and peat moss. They prefer partial shade, as the leaves can scald in the bright sun. Mulch twice a year with compost or well-rotted manure. Keep the soil moist. Indoors, keep the humidity level high with a commercial humidifier or by setting the pots in a flat container filled with pebbles. Add water to the top of the pebbles and let evaporate, refilling as necessary. They are hardy to Zone 8.

GLADIOLUS TRISTIS

THIS GLADIOLUS differs greatly from the common gladiolus in several ways. Of most interest to evening gardeners is its sweet fragrance, which is more pronounced in the evening than during the day.

Unlike most gladiolus, which have swordlike leaves, this native of South Africa has nearly cylindrical erect leaves that twist into spirals. They

Its flowers open white and age to deep golden yellow.

'Mystery' is the best-known variety. It grows 6 to 8 feet tall and produces impressive 4- to 5-inch flowers in spring and early summer.

'Radicans' is a 12-inch-high minia-

should be shown off in the evening garden, either by subtly lighting the plant or silhouetting it against a white wall.

The flower spikes grow 18 to 24 inches tall. The yellowish-white veined blossoms are about 2 inches long and often have throats suffused with purple.

In warm areas, plant the corms in late winter 3 inches deep and 3 inches apart in full sun and well-drained soil. In colder areas, it is best to grow this gladiolus as a pot plant in a greenhouse.

KAHILI GINGER— HEDYCHIUM GARDNERANUM

I FIRST SAW this plant at South Coast Botanical Garden, south of Los Angeles, at sunset. The exotic flowers caught the last rays of the sun, luring me toward the plant. As I got closer, I slowly became enveloped in a sweet, rich fragrance. I was mentally transported to a remote Pacific island, surrounded by these magnificent plants. I was soon back to the reality of southern California smog, but grateful for the brief vacation in my mind.

This exotic perennial, which may grow up to 8 feet tall, has broad 8- to 18-inch-long leaves that grow on two sides of the stems in a single plane and an imposing 14-inch-long spike of fragrant flowers. The flowers are clear lemon-yellow with long, prominent red stamens. In late summer or early fall, the dense, richly fragrant spike of flowers opens from a cone of overlapping green bracts

at the ends of the stalks.

Place kahili ginger in a container next to other tropical-looking plants such as palms, ferns or cycads to create the illusion of a tropical paradise, even in suburbia, and let its aroma transport you to a faraway vision of paradise.

Grow in light shade in rich soil enriched with organic matter. Keep consistently moist. Cut back the stems after the flowers fade to encourage new growth. It is hardy in parts of the Southwest. Grow as a container plant elsewhere.

JASMINE (ARABIAN JASMINE)— JASMINUM SAMBAC

I FINALLY SUCCEEDED in growing jasmine in my sunroom. I have had the plant for two years, but this is the first year it has bloomed.

When I first got my jasmine, my husband placed it against a window where it caught a chill and lost all its buds. The next year, it was growing well and my expectations were high. It had lovely foliage that crept across the table, looking for a place to climb. It set bud, and just as the first

white star-shaped flower opened, I left on a two-week trip. I had completely forgotten about it until I returned and stepped into a sweet, exotic cloud of fragrance. It was winter outside, but in that room, it smelled like a tropical evening.

Arabian jasmine is an evergreen vining plant. In all but the warmest areas, where it may be grown outdoors, it can easily be grown as a winter-blooming houseplant. It is one of the oldest jasmine species in cultivation.

Arabian jasmine's deep green leaves are opposite each other, sometimes in leaflets of three. The tubular white flowers are borne in clusters in the winter and are intensely fragrant. 'Maid of Orleans' is an excellent new cultivar.

Keep jasmine lightly moist in spring and summer. Feed every two weeks. In fall and winter, allow the soil to dry out a bit between waterings. During the drier period, do not fertilize. In spring, prune the stems back and repot, using an all-purpose potting mix. Jasmine can be propagated from tip cuttings in summer or fall.

Jasmine grows best in bright light, with several hours of full sun each day. It prefers 60-degree F nights and 80-degree F days. It is hardy only in Zone 10.

SWEET PEA— LATHYRUS ODORATUS

THE UNIQUE SCENT of sweet pea—honeylike with a citrus overtone—is a delightful addition to the evening garden in spring. Sweet pea is a vinelike annual that grows 4 to 6 feet long. The flowers look like pea flowers—they are of the same family, but this plant is poisonous. The 2-inch flowers are usually borne in clusters of three to five.

There are numerous cultivated varieties that include dwarf, heat-resistant, nonclimbing and early-flowering types. There is also a wide range of colors—scarlet, crimson,

rose, salmon, medium blue, light blue, lavender and white. The purple flowers of the old-fashioned cultivars are most fragrant.

Like the edible pea, the sweet pea is a cool-season plant. It thrives in spring, but begins to fade as the mercury climbs.

Sow seeds outdoors in full sun as soon as the soil can be worked in spring. To lengthen the season, apply a mulch of clear plastic over previously prepared soil in late winter. Plant the seeds through slits in the plastic. Allow four to six seeds per foot. When the plants are about 2 inches high, cover the plastic with grass clippings. In mild areas, plant the seeds in late fall for a spring bloom. Provide support for most varieties.

HONEYSUCKLE
(WILD HONEYSUCKLE,
JAPANESE HONEYSUCKLE)—
LONICERA JAPONICA

THE SWEET SCENT of honeysuckle transports me back to the warm summer nights of my childhood. After dinner, we used to walk the dog, often passing a park where honeysuckle grew wild. Its sweet fragrance was wondrous. My father showed me how to suck the nectar from the plant: Carefully snapping a tiny piece at the base of the flower without breaking the filament, I slowly pulled the piece away from the flower, bringing the filament toward me. Then out popped a drop of golden nectar that I touched to my tongue. What a

sensual delight.

Japanese honeysuckle was imported into America from Japan around the turn of the century. It is often described as an evergreen twining vine that climbs or covers the ground and self-roots as it goes. This slightly hairy vine can easily grow to 30 feet in length. The 2- to 3-inch-long narrow heart-shaped leaves are deep green and often downy below, but less commonly downy above.

The flowers appear in May and continue to bloom sporadically through late summer. When the first flush of bloom is on the vine, the scent wafts through the air, especially at night. That is the time to discover where honeysuckle is growing—its sweet perfume will lead you to the plant. The flowers are trumpet-shaped and grow in pairs.

Winter honeysuckle, *Lonicera fragrantissima*, blooms in late winter to early spring and has smaller inedible flowers. Its fragrance is very lemony and delicious, especially during this bleak period in northern gardens. It is hardy to Zone 5.

There is more information in the literature on how to control and eradicate Japanese honeysuckle than there is on how to grow it. Although it is beautiful on a trellis or bower, the risk is too great that this plant will get out of bounds. Once it escapes, it can spread rapidly to open sunny areas, strangling anything in its path. If you already have it growing in your garden you may as well enjoy it. Unfortunately, it is too rangy to grow well in a container.

The honeylike scent of sweet pea, **opposite,** *is a good addition to the spring garden.* **Below:** *Honeysuckle in bloom.*

OLEANDER (ROSE BAY)—
NERIUM OLEANDER

I FIRST SMELLED oleander at the Getty Museum in Malibu, California. Now I recognize and enjoy its light scent when I drive around southern California in the evening. Although it is commonly used in landscapes and even as a street tree, I was pleasantly surprised to find that, even in a mass planting, its perfume is not overwhelming. But beware, although its odor is welcoming the plant itself is poisonous.

Oleander, with its light scent, is a perfect addition to a warm-climate evening garden. Although the plant can get large, it is not overpowering—it grows from 8 to 20 feet tall.

Oleander is an ornamental evergreen shrub or small tree that is seen mostly in the South and West. The narrow 4- to 10-inch leaves are

Its warm but not overwhelming scent makes oleander a perfect addition to a garden in the South or West.

somewhat thick and leathery. They are dark green above and pale below with a prominent lower midrib.

Uplighting oleander shows off the attractive pale undersides of the leaves. The pink, white, red, purple or yellow fragrant flowers are funnel-shaped and borne in showy terminal clusters.

Oleander is tolerant of drought, heat and salt. It grows best in well-drained soil in a hot, sunny spot. To keep it in shape, prune it in early spring. It is hardy throughout much of the South and West.

HOLLY OSMANTHUS (HOLLY OLIVE)— OSMANTHUS HETEROPHYLLUS

MANY OF THE flowers that perfume the evening garden are at their peak in the warm weather of summer. Once the days and nights start getting frosty in autumn, most of the plants go into dormancy or die. Holly osmanthus is there to add its sweet honeylike aroma to the evening garden in autumn.

I first smelled osmanthus while wandering through a friend's Pennsylvania garden late one afternoon. It was a chilly, damp day and a scent that seemed out of place with its warmth wafted toward me. I was drawn to a handsome broad-leaved evergreen—the source of the delightful scent. It was not a plant I knew—my friend introduced it as holly osmanthus.

Holly osmanthus is an evergreen shrub that grows 15 to 20 feet tall with 1½- to 2½-inch oblong leaves. Some leaves have marginal spines, like holly leaves, while others are rounded. Osmanthus blooms in mid to late fall. The flowers are white in 1- to 1½-inch-long clusters.

This shrub is excellent as a single plant, but it may also be used as a hedge or an espalier. It grows best in acid soil and partial shade and is hardy to Zone 7.

MIGNONETTE–
RESEDA ODORATA

IT IS NOT the most attractive plant, yet an evening garden would not be the same without the clean, fresh scent of mignonette. I am not ashamed to admit I stick mignonette here and there in the garden, tucked in with other plants that to me are more attractive. I am still rewarded with its fragrance, without giving it a prime spot in the garden.

Mignonette is an annual that grows about 12 inches tall. Stout oval spikes rise above somewhat coarse foliage bearing numerous tiny yellow or reddish flowers. Individually, the flowers are inconspicuous, and the plant as a whole is not much to look at.

For prolonged bloom, plant mignonette outdoors in early spring and again in late summer. Mignonette grows best in rich garden soil in full sun to partial shade. It does not transplant well. Sow seeds directly in the garden, barely covered with soil, as the seeds need light to germinate.

LILAC–SYRINGA VULGARIS

MANY COMMONLY grown plants work well in the evening garden. The common lilac is one of these. Their fragrance is incomparable on warm spring evenings and their range of colors make some visible at night. White and light purple or mauve lilacs are most visible, but also look for lilacs with variegated leaves for added interest.

The common lilac is native to southeastern Europe. It is a beautiful flowering shrub. Lilacs may grow, if unpruned, up to 15 feet tall, usually in shrub form. The heart-shaped leaves are an attractive green.

Lilacs are widely available in the nursery trade. Plant them in the

spring or fall. Suckers can be dug out and replanted in early fall. Allow at least 6 feet between plants. Mulch lilacs with 4 to 6 inches of well-rotted manure every two years in autumn.

Lilacs benefit from regular pruning. In the winter, remove all dead and weak wood that does not have large flower buds or that still has the previous year's fruit on it. In the spring, the number of blooms will not be great, but each cluster will be large. The second year, more and larger flowers will be produced. By the third year, the clusters will be more plentiful, but they will begin to get smaller. Repeat the pruning process every three years.

Lilacs prefer full sun but will tolerate partial shade. They grow in almost any soil type as long as it is well-drained and not acidic. Acidic soil will prevent flowering. Lilacs are hardy to Zone 4. Since they need a period of winter cold and dormancy, lilacs cannot grow in Zones 8 to 10.

LINDEN (BASSWOOD,
LIME TREE)–TILIA SP.

I HAD ALWAYS enjoyed the sweet perfume of lindens, but had never considered them for an evening garden until last summer.

At the end of a long tiring day, I was finally luxuriating in a hot tub at a bed and breakfast near Victoria, British Columbia. Suddenly, I became aware of the sweetness of the

Tilia americana will grow in a wide variety of soils.

air I was breathing. The scent was familiar, but its source eluded me.

The next morning, I saw a magnificent tree in a nearby field. As I walked toward the tree to identify it, I recognized the flowers and the scent—it was the linden that had perfumed the evening air.

Different linden species can interbreed, so it is common to find natural hybrids. For this reason, it may be difficult to identify the species of linden with complete accuracy. The American linden (*Tilia americana*) is native to most of the eastern half of North America. Other lindens include European linden (*Tilia* x *europaea*), small-leaved linden (*T. cordata*) and broad-leaved linden (*T. platyphyllos*).

Lindens are handsome deciduous trees, much prized as street trees, that grow 40 to 80 feet tall or more. The heart-shaped leaves have fine, sharp-toothed edges and range in size from 3 to 9 inches long. Small whitish to yellowish flowers appear in early summer. The flower stalk comes out of a leaflike bract.

Purchase a young tree from a reputable nursery in the spring or fall. Mulch well around the base of the tree, but not right up to the trunk. When planting a linden, take into account its ultimate size when planning nearby plantings.

All lindens need full sun. *T. americana* grows in a range of soils. *T. cordata* grows best in cool, deep, moist loam. *T. platyphyllos* prefers light soil and humid surroundings. Depending on the species, lindens are hardy from Zone 7 to 8.

Violets have become naturalized throughout much of North America.

SWEET VIOLET (ENGLISH VIOLET, GARDEN VIOLET)— VIOLA ODORATA

As I enter my driveway on a warm spring night, I can catch the sweet perfume of the violets. My headlights illuminate the pale delicate flowers, and I am often compelled to pick a bunch to place on my nightstand. The scent of violets seems old-fashioned to me—it reminds me of my grandmother. In spring, she would pick violets, then dry them to make sachets for her linen and lingerie drawers.

Violets have become naturalized throughout most of North America and have been cultivated for more than 2,000 years. They are creeping perennials whose dark green heart-shaped leaves grow low to the ground in rosettes.

The plant is only about 6 inches tall. The sweetly scented flowers, which appear singly on long stalks, range in color from deep violet to rose, white and mottled white.

Violets spread by runners called stolons. The easiest way to cultivate violets is to dig up one or more clumps from an existing area and transplant them in spring or fall.

Violets can also be grown from seed. Stratify the seeds by placing them in the refrigerator for several days. Sow outdoors in the spring or start them indoors 8 to 10 weeks before the last frost date. Violet seeds require darkness to germinate, so cover outdoor plantings with enough soil to eliminate the light. Place indoor seeds in a closet until they germinate (approximately one to three weeks). Transplant seedlings outdoors around the last frost date, allowing 5 to 8 inches between plants.

Violets grow best in partial shade. They will thrive even in poor soil, but for best results, plant them in fertile, moist, well-drained soil enriched with organic matter. They are hardy from Zone 5 to 9.

Stars of the Evening Garden

Night-blooming Cereus peruvianus bears 5-inch-diameter flowers.

O F ALL THE PLANTS and flowers, the "stars" are my favorites. Over the years, I have enjoyed them in my own garden and in those of others

The stars evoke a mood and bring a smile to my face when I recall their appearance and scent or come upon them in a garden or in the wilds. I also remember the people with whom I have shared the enjoyment of these plants and the special evenings that they made even more memorable.

GARLIC CHIVE (CHINESE CHIVE)— ALLIUM TUBEROSUM

T HE MOST STRIKING planting of garlic chives I have seen was in a 12-foot-long crescent-shaped garden. The garden was simply an edging of lamb's ears (another "star") filled in with garlic chives.

In late summer, the flower clusters caught the light of the moon as they swayed in the gentle breeze. The effect was that of a twinkling crescent moon on the ground that seemed to be a reflection of the one hanging in the evening sky. From that point on, I began to include garlic chives on my list of best choices for the evening garden.

Garlic chives are hardy perennial herbs with narrow, flattened gray-green leaves that grow about 12 inches tall. The leaves are grasslike in appearance, but are solid enough to stand upright.

Besides its use as an edible herb (the leaves have a lovely garlicky flavor), this is an attractive plant for a perennial border. The flower stalks reach 18 to 30 inches high and are topped with a flat-headed cluster of white flowers in midsummer. The bright flowers show up well against a dark background.

Plant garlic chives anytime from midspring through summer, allowing 12 inches between plants. The chives can be aggressive, so divide and thin plants whenever necessary.

If a plant starts to look too woody, trim the foliage back to within 1 inch of the ground. As traumatic as this trimming may seem, the chives will

Garlic chives, **below**, *are an attractive perennial for the border.* **Opposite:** *the artichoke's silver foliage stands out at night.*

benefit from such a severe pruning.

Do not allow garlic chives to go to seed in a perennial garden, or you will have seedlings coming up everywhere.

Garlic chives grow best in full sun in average garden soil. They are hardy to Zone 4.

NIGHT-BLOOMING CEREUS— CEREUS PERUVIANUS

I FIRST SAW this cereus growing at my aunt's house in southern California. I am not terribly fond of cacti, but this had a pleasing upright shape and blue-green color. However, that is all inconsequential—this cereus is grown for its magnificent flowers.

I was present when the first buds opened. At about 11 p.m., a bud expanded. Then the outer scales began to draw back, revealing the white petals beneath. Gradually, the petals pulled away from the bud until the entire flower had opened. It was magnificent.

By the next morning, the flower had already faded. Fortunately, there were several more buds, so we were treated to more flowers over a two-week period. One night, three flowers opened at once—what a spectacular sight.

This is one of the several plants that is called a night-blooming cereus. However, it is the only one that, botanically speaking, is a true cereus.

It is a tall, branching cactus with a treelike habit that can, under optimum conditions, reach 30 feet or more. Its body is ribbed with scattered spines.

In June, large white flowers (6 to 7 inches long and up to 5 inches across) open, each for just one night. Unlike other night-blooming cacti, all the flowers do not bloom simultaneously, so your chances of catching this cactus in the act are excellent.

Very few people live in a climate where they can grow this striking cactus outdoors. However, it is easily grown as a container plant, albeit a very large one.

Grow in full sun in well-drained soil. It is hardy in parts of the Southwest.

ARTICHOKE—CYNARA SCOLYMUS

WITH ITS BOLD, elaborately cut, silver-green foliage, the artichoke is a great plant for the evening garden. Not only does it show up well at night because of its coloration, but its form adds architectural interest year-round.

I have long admired artichokes in California gardens and have promised myself for many years that I would try my luck at growing one in my own garden. The problem is that they need so long a growing period (150 to 180 days to maturity). I never seem to get the plant ordered or the seed started early enough.

At last, I solved the problem. I brought a small plant home from

forming a plant that is almost as wide as it is tall.

Plant the artichoke in a 3-gallon container and grow it indoors in bright light until after the last frost in spring. Gradually harden the plants off and transplant them into the garden. Allow 4 feet between plants. Water frequently during dry spells. Mulch well to conserve water.

Artichokes grow best in full sun in fertile, sandy loam. They are typically grown in California, but will also grow well throughout the South and Southwest. In more northern areas, artichokes can only be grown as an annual with considerable effort.

ANGEL'S TRUMPET— DATURA METELOIDES (DATURA INOXIA)

No EVENING GARDEN should be without at least one datura. I had several on the property where I lived in Portugal. What magnificent plants they are—their sweet perfume is reminiscent of lilies mixed with daffodils. Several grew as volunteers in that warm climate, strategically located near the compost pile and outhouse, so that necessary visits to both places were more pleasant.

Angel's trumpet is stocky—it grows 3 to 4 feet tall and almost as wide. It is a tender perennial, but it is usually grown as a tender annual.

'Evening Fragrance' is a new hybrid with huge 8-inch pure white flowers with a soft lavender picotee

California this winter. I potted it up in a good-sized container and will keep it in my sunroom until late May, when it will go out into the garden.

In northern areas, artichokes can be grown from offsets or root divisions started indoors in midwinter. (Offsets can be purchased from the specialty growers listed in Sources & Further Reading, page 164.)

Most people grow the plant to harvest the edible artichokes, however, I will be pleased just to have the handsome plant in my garden.

The edible artichoke is actually the immature flower bud. The plant is outstanding for its foliage. The 3- to 5-foot-long leaves arch gracefully,

edging and slate blue foliage. The flowers are especially fragrant at night.

Angel's trumpet grows best in a large container. It is usually grown from seed. For autumn bloom, start seeds indoors in midwinter. Optimum germination occurs between 65 and 70 degrees F. Transplant outdoors into full sun several weeks after all danger of frost has passed. This plant is sensitive to cold, so move it indoors before the first frost.

DAPHNE 'CAROL MACKIE'— DAPHNE X BURKWOODII 'CAROL MACKIE'

DAPHNE 'CAROL MACKIE' is one of my all-time favorite plants, especially for an evening garden. It was one of the first plants I put in when I landscaped our landlady's swimming pool seven years ago.

Even when first planted at a size of no more than 12 inches, Daphne 'Carol Mackie' is a lovely shrub. I soon realized that it flowers in late May—just about the time when the pool is first swimmable.

During one of my moonlight swims, I noticed that the fragrance was even headier at night than during the day. What a delight it was to come up for air and drink in the sweet perfume of this beautiful plant. The temptation was great to just turn on my back and float in the

fragrance and let my mind wander.

This semievergreen shrub is attractive any time of the year. It has an erect habit and grows slowly to 4 feet tall and just as wide. It is densely branched with narrow, oblong, green leaves banded in pale gold that grow completely around each stem. This variegation is another plus in the evening garden as it is quite visible. In May and June, the shrub is covered with clusters of small, pale pink, star-shaped flowers.

Grow 'Carol Mackie' in humus-enriched soil in full sun or light shade. It is hardy from Zone 4 to 8.

SNOW-ON-THE-MOUNTAIN (GHOSTWEED)—EUPHORBIA MARGINATA

SNOW-ON-THE-MOUNTAIN, with its variegated foliage, is a great plant for the evening garden. The white edges of the leaves stand out, while the green portions disappear. With its many small leaves that catch the lightest breeze, from a distance at night it looks like hundreds of large fireflies congregated in one area of the garden.

Don't be disappointed, as I was the first time I grew snow-on-the-

Daphne 'Carol Mackie,' **top,** *is especially fragrant at night.* **Bottom:** *Snow-on-the-mountain.*

mountain. For months, I thought the seed company had made a mistake—the plants I had nurtured were growing lustily in my garden, but they were definitely green with no sign of variegation. Dejected, I

went away for a week at the end of July. When I returned, the snow-on-the-mountain was variegated, not solid green.

Snow-on-the-mountain is a handsome, fast-growing annual that grows to 3 feet tall. The first leaves to appear on the plant, which are the lower leaves, are large and green. It is not until late July or early August that the first variegated leaves appear—striking green leaves with white margins. Eventually, the upper branches with variegated leaves hide the plain green leaves below.

The bracts of the flower clusters are showy and white with small, greenish-white flowers in the center. Warning: The milky sap of this and other

euphorbias may be a skin irritant.

Snow-on-the-mountain is grown from seed. In areas with short summers, start indoors six weeks before the last frost date. In other areas, sow the seeds directly in the ground once the soil has warmed.

Grow in full sun in average soil. Thin as necessary to allow 24 inches between plants.

SUMMER HYACINTH (GIANT SUMMER HYACINTH)— GALTONIA CANDICANS

I REMEMBER SUMMER hyacinth from a friend's upstate New York garden in midsummer more than 20 years ago. A large clump was in bloom at the edge of the garden bordering a meadow. The sweet scent, suggestive of the spring-blooming hyacinth (no relation, but that is how it got its common name), coupled with the hanging white bell-shaped flowers attracted me immediately to the plant.

Unfortunately, my friend had been misinformed about the plant's name and told me it was a tuberose. For years I grew tuberoses, but they were never the same, and I could not understand why.

It was only recently, when I planted galtonia in my evening garden, that I had a clue as to the identity of the well-remembered plant. I was overjoyed when it bloomed in August—I had rediscovered a favorite plant from years before.

Galtonia is a summer-flowering bulb. The basal leaves are strap-shaped and grow 2 to 3 feet long.

The flowering stalk may grow 2 to 4 feet tall, with the flowers loosely clustered along the upper third of the stalk. The 1½-inch flowers are narrow and bell-shaped. They open over a period of weeks—those lower on the stalk open first—and fill the evening air with a fragrant scent.

Surround galtonias with low summer-flowering white dahlias or tall snapdragons—its gawkiness will be hidden and the blooming bells will suddenly look elegant.

In spring, once the soil has warmed, plant the bulbs 6 inches deep. Mulch with 2 inches of compost or organic matter every fall. In other areas, dig up the bulbs after the foliage has turned brown and store in sawdust or sand in a cool, dark area until spring.

Galtonia prefers rich, well-drained soil that has been amended with compost or well-rotted manure. It grows best in full sun and is hardy to Zone 6.

HELIOTROPE— HELIOTROPIUM ARBORESCENS

HELIOTROPE EARNS a place in the summer evening garden more for its scent than for any of its other attributes. The rich odor, reminiscent of violets with a vanilla overtone, is one of the quintessential smells of summer to me.

*Summer hyacinth, **left**, fills the evening air with a sweet scent.*
Right: *A heliotrope grows in front of an orange tree.*

Heliotrope grows best in full sun in northern areas. In the South and West, give it some afternoon shade. It prefers rich soil, but will grow in average garden earth.

HOSTA (PLANTAIN LILY, FUNKIA)—HOSTA SP.

I GREW UP WITH what we called funkia (now a more obscure common name for hosta). The heart-shaped, variegated, medium green-and-white leaves are stunning in late afternoon and evening. In August, a spike of pale lavender flowers rises above the leaves, perfuming the air. I was certainly surprised to learn, many years later, that funkia is another name for hosta.

Hostas are old-fashioned, easy-to-grow perennials that have never lost their popularity with gardeners. For years, hostas have been the mainstay of most shade gardens. They brighten and cheer up any dark spot.

Some hostas are more suited to an evening garden than others—ones with variegated leaves are choice as are varieties with fragrant and/or white flowers.

There are over 40 known species from which hundreds of hybrids have been developed over the years. All are prized for their handsome basal leaves in a variety of shapes, colors and sizes from the diminutive 'Thumb Nail,' with 1-inch leaves, to the might of 'Sum and Substance,' with its 2-foot heart-shaped light

It is amazing how a single whiff of the flower, even one growing in a greenhouse, is enough to evoke memories of hot summer nights long ago. If the fragrance is not enough to endear this plant to evening gardeners, the white-flowered variety is visible at night and the more common purple variety fluoresces in the late-afternoon light.

Heliotrope grows up to 4 feet tall in mild climates and has a somewhat shrubby form. Modern hybrids are shorter, ranging from 18 to 24 inches high. The leaves are slightly hairy and have a darkish-purple cast. The small, dark purple and sometimes white flowers are tightly grouped on

one-sided spikes that form rounded, massed clusters of bloom.

It is a heat-loving plant that thrives in the dog days of summer. While everyone else is wilting on a hot humid night, bend down and take a whiff of the heliotrope and you will have visions of homes with wrap-around porches, squeaky swings and blue-painted ceilings, and perhaps even the sensation of sipping an icy mint julep.

Start seeds indoors 10 to 12 weeks before the last frost date. Seeds germinate best in a warm environment of 70 to 75 degrees F. Transplant them into the garden several weeks after all danger of frost has passed.

green leaves and lavender flowers that bloom in late summer.

The leaves may be a solid color, variegated or a blend of two colors— deep green, cream, white, chartreuse, blue-green or pale green. The flowers are a bonus, rising on stalks above the neat mound of leaves from mid-summer to autumn. Some flowers, such as the double flowers of *Hosta plantaginea* 'Aphrodite,' are extremely showy and fragrant.

Most hostas grow best in partial shade, although some varieties will grow in full sun in northern gardens. In general, varieties with blue foliage do best in shade, those with yellow foliage like partial shade to full sun, and variegated hostas perform best in light shade to full sun. For the best effect, plant in groups of three.

Hostas prefer rich soil amended with organic matter. Keep well watered during the heat of summer. They are hardy from Zone 3 to 9, depending on the variety.

MOONFLOWER— IPOMOEA ALBA

I HAVE MOONFLOWERS trained around the entrance to my home. The flowers are a cheery greeting when I come home in the evening. They are also a fragrant welcome for guests, always providing a topic of conversation. When guests depart, I pluck a flower and give it to them for their journey home.

Each moonflower opens for just one night. It is a mesmerizing process to watch. The swollen, elon-gated bud seems to unfurl. Slowly, over a period of about 20 minutes, the bud opens to reveal a large 5- to 6-inch-wide white, almost iridescent flower that looks much like a morning glory, though, unlike a morning glory, it is fragrant. The flowers stay

Each moonflower opens for just one night. It is a mesmerizing process. The swollen bud seems to unfurl to reveal a large 5- to 6-inch-wide flower.

open through the night and do not close until after dawn when sunlight shines directly on them. On cloudy days, they sometimes remain open.

Moonflowers are the night-blooming cousins of morning glories. As morning glories open, moonflowers are closing after a long night of perfuming the air with their fragrance.

Moonflowers are annual twining vines native to tropical America. They flourish in the heat of summer. Though slow to get started, once the weather turns hot, the vines start climbing and run their way up the supports provided. For six or more weeks, depending on when the first frost strikes, the vine is in full flower. In areas where there is no frost, as the temperature cools, the vines die.

To expedite germination, soak the seeds in warm water overnight. Plant out in the garden when the soil temperature is consistently above 70 degrees F. They flourish in hot weather and warm soil, so be patient if the vines remain small for some time. Once the weather is warm enough, they will take off in a spurt.

Provide support with a trellis or an arbor as these vines easily grow to 10 feet or more and are quite heavy when they are laden with buds and flowers. Moonflowers will grow in most soils.

NIGHT-SCENTED STOCK— MATTHIOLA BICORNIS

NIGHT-SCENTED stock is considered by many to be the straggly cousin of the attractive stock commonly grown in the garden. However, any evening gardener knows that this diminutive plant is head and shoulders above its more majestic relative when it comes to fragrance.

This plant's flowers seem to exude the sweet scent of honey in the evening. Like mignonette, night-scented stock is not terribly showy. I prefer to tuck it in among unscented, showy plants like snapdragons and let the scent drift into the air.

Night-scented stock grows only 18 inches tall and has a straggly appearance. It bears small mauve mustardlike flowers that give off their characteristic scent from late afternoon well into the night.

The larger stocks (*Matthiola incana*) are annuals that are easy to grow and quick to flower. Unlike many other annuals, they are cold-resistant—they thrive in the cool of spring, but die back in the heat of summer.

There are many hybrid varieties of stock. They range in height from 8 to 30 inches and have single or double flowers borne in clusters that often cover most of the stem. Flowers range in color from white through blue, purple, carmine-red, rose, apricot and various bicolors.

Start stock seeds indoors in winter so that the plants are actually in bud when they are transplanted outdoors. An alternative is to plant seeds directly in the garden in very early spring. Sow the seeds thickly. Do not thin the plants, since the stress of crowding will cause them to bloom early. In areas with mild winters, sow the seeds outdoors in late summer and you will be rewarded with blooms throughout the winter and into spring.

FLOWERING TOBACCO— NICOTIANA ALATA NICOTIANA— NICOTIANA SYLVESTRIS

NICOTIANAS ARE true stars of the evening garden. The flowers are narrow tubes that flare out at the end to form a five-petaled star. During the day, the flowers droop. At night, the flowers revive and their sweet scent perfumes the air.

One of the most innovative uses of nicotiana I have seen was in a Connecticut garden, planted among ornamental grasses. The garden was naturalistic, resembling an overgrown meadow, so the sweet fragrance of the nicotiana was a good counterpoint.

Hybridizers have worked long and hard with *Nicotiana alata*, modifying it to create a "better" plant. In my opinion, the original plant is close to perfection. It has a rangy, airy form and a plenitude of fragrant white flowers that open in the evening and close in the morning. New cultivated varieties are more compact and colorful. Unfortunately,

During the day, the flowers of Nicotiana sylvestris appear to droop. At night, they revive and fill the air with sweet perfume.

their scent has been sacrificed in many cases.

Nicotiana alata, in its pure form, has a 15- to 18-inch basal rosette of dark green oval leaves. In early summer, each rosette produces a central stem that quickly grows 4 feet tall with secondary stems that eventually grow to 2 feet. The overall effect is of a giant candelabra with flowers in graceful sprays. It begins to flower in early July. Cut some to enjoy indoors—the pruning will stimulate the plant to produce more flowers.

Nicotiana sylvestris grows large rosettes of verdant green leaves up to 2 feet long and 1 foot across. By midsummer, it sends up a single 5- to 6-foot-high stalk. Large leaves grow intermittently on the stalk, each of which gives rise to a smaller-leaved side branch. At the end of each branch is a cluster, or "cob," of

as many as 50 flower buds.

From mid-July until frost, 4- to 5-inch-long chalk-white flowers are produced. The flowers hang down gracefully.

Many nicotianas are now available at nurseries or garden centers as small plants in late spring and early summer. An alternative is to grow them from seed.

Start seeds of this annual indoors in late winter or early spring. Transplant them into the garden after all danger of frost has passed. Allow 12 to 15 inches between larger varieties, 8 to 12 inches between smaller ones. Once you have grown nicotiana in your garden, you will be treated to self-sown seedlings in subsequent years.

Nicotianas are easy to grow. They prefer full sun, but will do fine in partial shade. They are not fussy about soil.

TROPICAL WATERLILIES—
NYMPHAEA SP.

D ON'T LET the name intimidate you. You don't need a pond, nor must you live in the tropics, to grow these aquatic additions to the evening garden. Although they are not winter-hardy, they can be either treated as annuals or overwintered indoors.

Tropical waterlilies have an exotic beauty and fragrance that add a touch of elegance to any garden. They are available in day- or night-blooming varieties. The large leaves, which may be solid green, bronze, maroon or mottled, float on the surface of the water. One plant may spread its leaves to cover 6 to 12 feet or more of the water surface.

The magnificent flowers, which grow up to 12 inches across, rise on erect stems above the water. Waterlilies will bloom from midsummer until frost.

You don't need to have a pond to grow waterlilies. Many varieties can be grown in containers, then submerged in large water-filled tubs. They need at least five or six hours of direct sunlight. Do not put them in the water until the water temperature is a constant 70 degrees F. They require still water 6 to 18 inches deep over the rootstock.

Allow at least 1 cubic foot of good, rich soil for each plant. Fertilize monthly with specially formulated food for water plants. They will thrive outdoors in summer only in Zones 3 to 10.

TUBEROSE—
POLIANTHES TUBEROSA

I LOVE THESE fragrant flowers in an evening garden because they bloom at a time when other flowers are beginning to fade—late summer and early fall.

I used to plant tuberose along with galtonia. Usually the galtonia is finished before the tuberose blooms, however one year they were out at the same time. The heady fragrance of the tuberose far outweighed the galtonia. Now I plant them at opposite ends of the garden, where they each can shine at night.

The botanical name of this late-summer-blooming bulb is derived from the Greek for "white, shining flowers," which describes the flowers well. The 2½-inch-long waxy white flowers are borne in short clusters at the end of the stalk. Although fragrant during the day, the flowers are even more aromatic at night.

The bright green basal leaves grow 12 to 18 inches long. Smaller leaves clasp the stem, which can grow to 3 feet tall. The flowers are the most interesting part of the plant, so plant a lower-growing annual or autumn-blooming perennial in front to hide the stem. Plant seven or more tuberoses in a group for impact.

Plant the tubers in a warm, sunny

Tropical waterlilies are available as day- or night-blooming varieties. **Left,** *waterlily 'Midnight.'*

location in rich, well-drained soil. Keep well watered during the growing season. Because of its height, this plant may need staking. Dig up the tubers before frost and overwinter them in a warm, dry place. They are hardy to Zone 9.

LAMB'S EARS—
STACHYS BYZANTINA
(STACHYS LANATA,
STACHYS OLYMPICA)

Ever since I was a child, I have been attracted to lamb's ears. The plant's soft, furry leaves beg to be stroked. Even though its leaves are silver-colored, I had not thought of it as an evening garden plant until I saw it edging a crescent-shaped garden filled with garlic chives. Then, I realized how perfect it was.

Lamb's ears grows 12 to 18 inches tall and spreads to form a thick mat of foliage. Its oblong leaves are covered with soft white hairs. Few people can pass a plant without stopping to touch it.

Some gardeners think its leafy flower spikes detract from the appearance of the plant. They may be removed, but I like the tiny splash of color the small purplish-pink flowers make in late spring and summer.

Lamb's ears is an excellent plant to use to edge a border, if you allow it enough room to sprawl. Once established in a garden, it self-seeds freely—providing you do not cut off the flower spikes. It is drought-tolerant. However, during hot, humid summers, it has a tendency to rot.

Lamb's ears is easy to grow. It

prefers full sun and average, well-drained soil. Sow seeds directly in the garden, spaced 12 inches apart, in early spring. It is hardy from Zone 4 to 10.

Tuberoses, **top,** *bloom in the late summer and fall.* **Bottom:** *Lamb's ears make an excellent border plant.*

Lighting

❧

OST GARDENERS I KNOW are more comfortable with a trowel than with a pair of wire cutters and a roll of electrician's tape. However, garden lighting should not be intimidating, even to an amateur. In my own garden, I started with some lighting to accent the mature oaks in my backyard. Over the years, I have added lights to other parts of the garden—in and around the swimming pool and

a few by what is now the edible-flower garden. Although you may have some ideas as to what you want for lighting, investigate the different techniques, fixtures and lamps (bulbs) before deciding on your plan. Ask yourself when you will be viewing the garden. From late afternoon into twilight, nature provides marvelous light, so no artificial enhancement is needed. After twilight, shadows, forms and plant colors come into play.

Without artificial lighting, the garden has a constantly changing look, depending on the amount of ambient light. After sunset, light may be reflected into the garden from indoors, neighbors' lights or street lights. The most variable light is moonlight—it is not only affected by lunar cycles, but by weather as well.

Lighting History

N 1898, James Breese commissioned Stanford White and Charles McKim, of the famed architectural firm McKim, Mead & White, to create a summer house for his family. It took eight years to transform 16 acres of woodland and potato fields in Southampton, New York, into the resulting masterpiece. The garden was nearly ½ mile long and about 500 feet wide. It was divided into an outer and an inner area. The inner garden was next to the house and surrounded on

Modern, low-voltage systems can make garden lighting unintimidating.

three sides by pergolas.

In 1916, Breese's inner garden was first bathed in artificial light. It was a tremendous undertaking. The effect of moonlight was created using special glass reflectors backed with silver to withstand the heat of 67,000 candlepower thrown by horizontal lights along the pergolas. A total of 500,000 candlepower illuminated the garden. Other cleverly concealed lights near the ground played through colored glass. Still more lights from the roof of the house illuminated the foliage and shrubbery in the garden.

Breese would marvel if he could see the miniaturization that has occurred in the field of lighting in the last few years. Until recently, all outdoor lighting was supplied by household current (120 volts). Installations had to be made by licensed electri-cians. Fixtures were often expensive and, unless custom-designed, not terribly imaginative.

Depending on code requirements, 120-volt lines have to be buried 12 to 24 inches underground. In many areas, they must be run in a rigid conduit. Once an installation is complete, it is not an easy matter to modify or change the design.

Over the last decade, low-voltage lights have become popular. The 12-volt outdoor lighting system evolved from the familiar automotive lighting system, which runs on 12 volts.

There are many advantages to low-voltage lights: The wire is buried only 6 inches deep; there is no need for a conduit, so the system is flexible; and the range of fixtures is tremendous. The one requirement is a step-down transformer to supply the system and transform 120-volt line current to a safe 12 volts.

In the last few years, several companies, such as Toro and Intermatic (see Sources & Further Reading, page 164) have come out with do-it-yourself low-voltage lighting kits, including transformers. These fixtures are relatively easy to install. Neither an engineering degree nor an electrician's license is necessary. The drawback is that most of the fixtures are plastic and may not prove as durable over time as metal fixtures.

Lighting Design

WHETHER YOU are tackling your lighting plan on your own or using a lighting designer, there are some straightforward prin-

ciples you should keep in mind. Decide what you want to illuminate in the hardscape. Do you want to draw attention to an interesting building, an attractive wall, an arbor, a gazebo or a fountain? Is it necessary to illuminate a path to invite strollers into the garden or to make the walk safe? What plants should be highlighted and to what degree? Are there aspects of the garden that you wish to minimize? What is the overall effect you want to create?

Keep in mind that the human eye perceives the light that is reflected off an object (reflectance). This is especially important to remember when creating a well-lighted garden, as light may be diverted by leaves, branches or other objects.

Consider the density of the leaves of the plant you intend to light—some leaves are translucent, while others allow no light to pass through them. Smooth shiny leaves reflect more light than wrinkled hairy leaves. White or light-colored objects have a greater reflectance than dark objects.

Your perception of the intensity of the light is also influenced by where you are standing. If you are indoors looking out at an illuminated garden, you get a lot of reflectance from the glass. The larger the window you are looking through, the more reflections come into play to distract you from the view outdoors. The brighter the

light where you are standing, the brighter the light has to be outside for you to perceive it.

To get the most out of a garden viewed from both indoors and out, a lighting system should have two levels of light—bright for viewing from indoors and less intense for viewing from outdoors. The two levels can be controlled by a dimmer switch or by having two-stage lighting.

Designing with light is like painting—you are creating a scene. Keep design basics in mind. Combine different lighting techniques—uplighting, downlighting and path lighting—to create the most interesting scene.

Strive for balance. Work on the largest and brightest lights first, then go on to the smaller lights to create a balance between light and dark. Observe the garden as you add and subtract lights. You may find you need more or fewer than you originally planned.

Lighting should subtly call attention to different facets of the garden—it should not be overwhelming. It is best to limit yourself to one or

two types of lamps. Different lamps have subtle color variations that can clash if they are not used properly. Before each fixture is permanently installed, walk around and through the illuminated garden and check for glare and eye comfort.

Unless you are using decorative fixtures, try to conceal the source of the light. This will enhance the magical effect of the lighting.

Make the design as flexible as possible, so you can easily adjust the lighting as plants grow. Consider mounting fixtures, especially for downlighting, on adjustable posts. With 12-volt lighting systems, leave several feet of extra wire at the base of each fixture to allow for movement as it becomes desirable.

If you have a complex lighting plan, consult a professional. A lighting designer can help you avoid some of the pitfalls, even if you are not doing a large design. A designer has a wide range of fixtures and lamps that you can try. Ask to see them at night; you cannot properly judge a light in the store. If you choose a 12-volt system, you may be able to install it yourself. If not, ask the designer for tips.

After you have lived with the garden for a while, you will have a better sense of the focal points you want to highlight, such as large trees, specimen plants or art objects. Decide which elements should be emphasized and, most importantly, from what points they will be viewed before you install lighting.

If trees have an open growth habit, allow light to spill through the branches and allow the leaves to create intriguing shapes and contrasts of light and shadow. If the foliage on the tree is full, try crosslighting or using a light that barely grazes the branches with its beam. If the tree has an unusual or interesting bark, graze the bark with light to accent the texture of the surface.

Don't overlook hanging plants and bonsais as focal points. Try silhouetting them or lighting them from behind to project a large shadow from a small plant. When lighting an art object, try to accentuate the effect the artist is trying to create with the piece.

Lighting Techniques

UPLIGHTING

THIS TECHNIQUE is often used to accent trees, shrubs and areas of architectural interest in the hardscape. Typically, the light fixture—usually a floodlight or spotlight—is placed at ground level and shines up at an object from below.

In nature, light always shines down from above. Uplighting is most unnatural, which makes it most dramatic. This technique is effective when the light beams up at an object at least 3 feet tall. The effect is not noticeable on shorter objects, unless they are viewed from below, such as from a lower terraced area or downhill.

Uplighting works best on plants that have great depth and open space, such as deciduous trees in the winter. It would not work well on a plant that has dense foliage, since the light could not visibly penetrate the lower level of foliage.

When considering uplighting, gauge the reflectance of the object you intend to feature, as the result of your efforts will be determined by this property. For example, the effect of lighting a white birch from below is quite striking because of its bark; uplighting a river birch with its smooth, shiny, reddish-brown bark is eye-catching, but more subtle. Plants whose leaves are lighter-colored on the underside may also be effectively accented from below.

Grazing is a form of uplighting used to emphasize surface textures, such as an interesting tree bark or a brick wall. In this technique, lights are positioned to rake over the surface—just close enough to create a pattern of light and shadow without blasting the surface and eliminating the drama of the shadows.

Mirroring relies on water to create a dramatic effect. Try uplighting an object near the edge of a moonlit lake. A pond or dark-bottomed pool will also work as long as the water is still and the entire reflection of the object can be seen. Trees and plantings on the opposite side of the water from the viewer can also be lighted to reflect on the dark surface of the water.

Perspective lighting is an excellent technique for creating the illusion of a larger area than really exists. It tricks the viewer's eye into believing that the end of the landscape is farther away than it actually is. The ef-

Shadowing is created when a light shines in front of a plant.

fect is achieved by uplighting on either side of a line of sight that serves as a corridor, such as a long narrow patio or a natural view through an allée. The most dramatic results are attained by dimly lighting the foreground, using a row of inground lights along the line of sight and spotlighting the focal point at the end of the sight line.

Shadowing is a technique that adds another kind of interest. When a light source is placed in front of a plant that is backed by a white wall, the enlarged shadow projected onto the wall is striking. Experiment with the placement of the light—placing it at an angle in front of the tree increases the size of the shadow and creates a more unusual backdrop.

You can also create shadowing on a translucent vertical surface, such as white Plexiglas or plastic, a Japanese shoji screen or other partially transparent item. This time, the effect is created in reverse. The screen is closest to the observer. The plant is behind the screen and the light hits the plant from behind. Items close to the screen will be smaller and have a sharp outline. Items farther away will be larger and less discernible.

Silhouetting (also known as backlighting) is a special uplighting technique. Place a floodlight at ground level between a plant and a wall or other vertical surface. Aim the light up toward the wall. The effect created is dramatic, especially if plants with uniquely shaped leaves or interesting branch formations are silhouetted. Be sure to conceal the light source in the ground or place it directly behind the object being silhouetted.

Spotlighting focuses an intense beam of light to accentuate a particular landscape detail or object, such as a fountain or statue. Spotlighting alone can ruin the subtle beauty of an evening garden, but by combining it with other lighting techniques, the potential for glare is greatly reduced. Try spotlighting objects from both above and below.

DOWNLIGHTING

Downlighting is the most natural looking lighting technique, since it imitates the light created by the sun and moon. Suspend concealed light sources above the garden. Direct the light straight down through trees and plant material.

Sidelighting is best used to illuminate paths, borders and driveways.

Contour lighting is a style of downlighting that uses low, hooded fixtures, such as mushroom or tier lights, to emphasize low plant forms and structures. This technique works well to highlight ground covers and flower beds. It is also good for defining path borders and reflecting pools.

Crosslighting is used to add depth and dimension to an object. To accomplish this, cross two or more floodlight beams high above an object. This creates softer shadows and a gentler effect than a single fixture would provide.

Moonlighting at its best duplicates the soft, diffused light of the full moon shining down on the garden, creating light and shadow as it filters through the trees. The effect is mystical, and it is easy to achieve. Position light fixtures high above the ground—the higher the better. Avoid lights that are too bright, or the scene will look theatrical. As with other lighting techniques, it is important to keep the source of the light out of view.

SIDELIGHTING (PATH LIGHTING)

Sidelighting, or path lighting, is best used to illuminate driveways, borders, paths and walkways. It is also effective for lighting low shrubbery and decorative ground

covers. With properly spaced fixtures, path lighting encourages you to explore the landscape, drawing you in to areas of interest.

Sidelighting is actually a form of downlighting, using lamps that have a wide light spread. It produces symmetrical patterns of illumination around the fixture. The fixtures are relatively low to the ground, usually no more than 2 to 2½ feet high, and may be shielded to diffuse the light and reduce glare.

When deciding on placement, keep safety in mind. How much light is needed for someone to walk through the area safely at night. Also consider the reflectivity of the plant material or pathway and the mood you are trying to establish. One striking effect is created when light fixtures are used on relatively open areas, where the plant growth does not interfere with the circles of light.

The Lamps

WHEN YOU THINK about lighting, it is often the fixture that comes to mind rather than the lamp, or bulb. Although the fixture may be decorative, it is the bulb within that truly creates the atmosphere.

Lamps are rated with a Color Rendition Index, or CRI. The higher the

Post lights are both attractive and versatile. They are often used for safety near entryways and along paths and driveways.

CRI, the more natural the light.

Halogen lamps have the highest CRI and are the brightest lamps. They are compatible with both 12-volt and 120-volt systems. Although more expensive than incandescent lamps, they are longer lasting and most efficient per watt consumed.

Incandescent lamps have a warm, almost honeylike color. They are compatible with both 12-volt and 120-volt systems. If insects are a problem, try installing yellow-tinted lamps instead of standard incandescent lamps. Insects are less attracted to these lights, but the color they project is definitely yellow, which may not be desirable.

Mercury vapor lamps give off a cool blue-green light. They are well suited for moonlighting as they illuminate a landscape in a realistic manner. They are also effective for downlighting and uplighting tall trees. Mercury vapor lamps are very long lasting (up to 20,000 hours), but they must be run on 120 volts. The fixtures can be somewhat bulky, as a ballast makes up a large part of the base. They are also significantly more expensive than halogen or incandescent lamps.

High-pressure sodium lamps give a yellow-pink cast. They last up to five years, but they are very expensive and have a bulky ballast. Low-pressure sodium lamps are now commonly used for street lighting and look just like the yellow of a traffic light. They have the lowest CRI of any lamp and everything looks brown under them. Sodium vapor lamps run only on 120-volt lines.

Light Fixtures

TODAY, THERE IS wide range of low-voltage outdoor lighting fixtures. Choosing a fixture is not just a matter of picking the most pleasing shape, color, size and material. Select the fixture whose design is best suited to the lighting technique it will be used for.

Custom-made fixtures are not necessarily expensive. If you are interested in custom fixtures, try contacting someone who does metalwork. If you have an idea in mind, they may be able to create the fixtures for less than you think.

Bollard lights have a contemporary look and are usually used for path lighting. Like post lights, they are either cylindrical or rectangular and are typically no more than 3 feet tall. Plastic or glass panels encase the lamp. Some bollard lights have shields that may be attached to direct the light to either side.

Bullet lights are the simplest housing for a lamp. They enclose the lamp in a cylindrical metal or plastic shield. The shield cuts down on glare and protects the lamp and socket from debris and moisture. Many bullet lights have glass or plastic lenses to further protect the lamp. Bullet lights are used for both uplighting and downlighting.

Floodlights emit a wide, powerful beam of light. The lamps are mounted in round or rectangular plastic or metal housings that are more utilitarian than decorative.

Tier lights, **top,** *project a soft, luminous ring on the ground.* **Bottom:** *A variable-control floodlight allows adjustment of the beam size.*

Some have recessed lamps to cloak and protect the light source. Floodlights are most often used for uplighting and downlighting.

Floodlights may be mounted at ground level and aimed upward or attached to a wall, a fence or an individual tree. A recent innovation is a variable-control floodlight that allows you to adjust the beam size from a wide floodlight to a tightly focused

Mushroom light cast a wide circle of light downward, illuminating a large area near their bases.

spotlight. Some manufacturers produce rectangular lights that rotate, which allows you to choose between a horizontal and a vertical beam.

Globe lights are generally used to sidelight paths, walkways and low-growing plants. A frosted or translucent sphere sits atop a post, so that light spreads over a large area without producing glare. In addition to providing soft light, globe lights are interesting forms in the hardscape.

Mushroom lights are shaped like toadstools or capped mushrooms. They are primarily used to illuminate paths, walkways, borders, low-growing plants and ground covers. Their shade conceals the light source and a wide circle of light spreads down-

ward, illuminating a relatively large area. If you like the look of a mushroom fixture, but want more focused lighting, a prismatic lens may be placed around the lamp, which cuts down on the area of illumination.

Post lights are very versatile and are commonly used for safety lighting near entryways and along paths and driveways. They usually range in height from 3 to 8 feet tall and are most often rectangular, but sometimes cylindrical. They are made of wood, plastic or metal. The lamp is at the top of the post, safely enclosed in a globe or chimney. Consider employing a light-diffusing material for the globe or chimney to reduce glare, especially when the lamp is at eye-level.

Tier lights have a classic design and are best suited to sidelighting paths, steps and low-growing plants. The tiers shine light downward and project a soft, luminous ring onto the ground. The glare from the light is softened by the tiers.

Most lighting fixtures are installed above ground. Inground lights or well lights are set below-grade or underground. Since they normally cast their light directly upward, they are used to uplight trees and shrubs. This form of lighting is useful when you wish to conceal the light source.

Inground lighting is especially effective for lighting an object that is viewed from all directions, since it minimizes the glare from all sides. During the daytime, these fixtures are not a visible distraction in the landscape, especially when placed in a low-growing ground cover. Several

manufacturers have well lights that swivel on their bases, which allows you to direct the light upward and at an angle.

Special Effects

WATER

UNDERWATER LIGHTING fixtures are available in a broad range of styles and prices. When lighting a pool or pond, it is important that the water be clear, as murky water is very unattractive, especially when lit.

When dealing with electricity and water, call in a professional to avoid any problems. Careful adherence to electrical codes will lengthen the life of a fixture and ensure greater personal safety.

LUMINARIAS

LUMINARIAS ARE wonderful for festive party lighting. They are inexpensive and easy to make—a small paper bag, sometimes with cut-out designs, is filled with 1 or 2 inches of sand into which a small votive candle is inset.

There is really no safety problem with these lights. The candle will burn out in the sand, and the bag provides protection from the wind. Sometimes a strong breeze will blow out the candles in perforated bags, so they may require constant relighting. For a dramatic effect, luminarias are best displayed closely spaced or massed in groups.

Lighting the Lights

THERE ARE A NUMBER of devices you can install that will automatically control the lights in your garden.

Electrical timers may be installed on 12-volt and 120-volt systems to turn lights on and off at preset times. A timer allows you the security of lights when you want them on without the expense of a light sensor.

A number of manufacturers have made transformers with built-in light sensors. When the natural outdoor light dims, the installed lights automatically turn on. If you are concerned about security, sensors will guarantee that your lights are working from dusk to dawn. A manual override switch is convenient if you do not want the lights to go on when you are away or if you want to turn out the lights when you go to bed.

If you only want the lights on when someone is actually in the garden or if you only want a small area lit at one time, consider installing motion detectors or heat sensors. Motion detectors or heat sensors may be set to a range of sensitivities and detectable heights so that animals walking in their path will not activate the system.

If you have a long path winding through the garden, you might have motion detectors positioned so that only 10 or 15 feet of path in front of you is illuminated and the lights extinguish after you have walked past.

James Breese started the exploration into garden lighting less than 100 years ago. His guests were impressed by what they saw, but it was only a daytime garden illuminated at night. Imagine what they could have created using all the elements of a modern evening garden.

Lighting can be as simple as a few spotlights or as elaborate as that of the Butchart Gardens' Italian Garden, **below.**

CHAPTER 5

Plans for Your Evening Garden

❧

WITH THE VARIETY of plant material and types of gardens, you should find inspiration for your own garden in the plans that follow. Feel free to combine ideas from several of the gardens into your design, or use one as the model for your garden. Pat Lanza owns and runs Shandelee Herb Gardens. Her Evening Garden (page 158) is a free-form kidney shape, surrounded by lawn. It is in hardiness zones

3 and 4. Betty Pruehsner designed her White Garden (page 159) for a small backyard typical of the walled and fenced yards in condominium complexes, townhouses and small suburban lots. It was created as a low-maintenance garden for people who have little time for gardening, yet want space for outdoor entertaining. Pruehsner's garden was designed for Zones 5 to 7.

In my own Crescent Moon Garden (page 160), both the lamb's ears and bamboo give the garden shape in winter as well as the rest of the year. The dwarf conifers provide vertical points of interest. The spring bulbs draw you out to the garden early in the season, and the tuberoses that follow perfume the air in late summer to fall. The evening primroses

open on summer nights. The trellises of moonflowers add a nice vertical accent and are showy from midsummer to frost.

Cathy's Corner (page 161) is my name for the evening garden right outside my house on the north shore of Long Island. It is an L-shaped garden that abuts the house and is bordered by a flagstone terrace.

Wood hyacinth with Forget-me-not, **above.**
Opposite: *Pat Lanza's Garden.*

The volume of plant material in Old Westbury Gardens' Grey Garden (page 162) may be too much for the recreational gardener. However, it provides a living synopsis of the gray- and silver-leaved plants best suited for its area in Zone 6.

Evening Garden

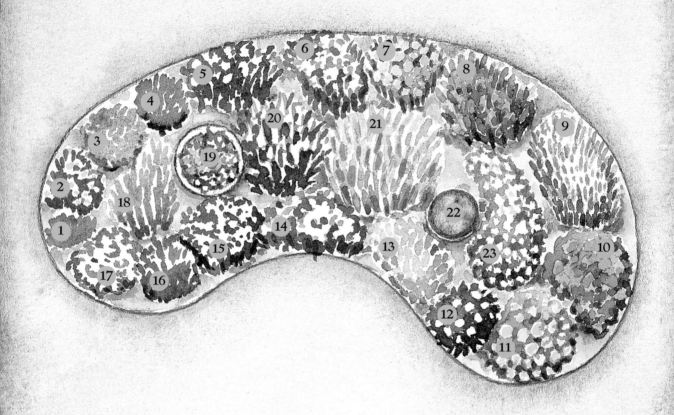

1. Longwood Thyme
2. 'Mt. Hood' Daffodil
3. 'Silver Mound' Artemisia
4. Silver Horehound
5. 'Sterling Star' Lily
6. Shasta Daisy
7. Cosmos
8. Kansas Gayfeather
9. Gooseneck Loosestrife
10. Garden Phlox
11. Cinquefoil
12. White Peony
13. Lamb's Ears
14. White Bee Balm
15. 'The Pearl' Yarrow
16. 'Bridal Veil' Garden Spirea
17. White Alyssum
18. 'Silver King' Artemisia
19. Annuals planted in tub:
    'White Orbit' Geranium
    'Snowdrift' Petunia
    'Snowfire' Dianthus
    Snapdragon
20. White Russell Lupine
21. 'Silver King' Artemisia
22. Garden Statuary
23. Feverfew

Designed by Pat Lanza

White Garden

1. Bradford Pear
2. Ground Cover*
3. Variegated Creeping
   Euonymus
4. Climbing Hydrangea
5. Ground Cover*
6. Korean Dogwood
7. White Wisteria
8. Ground Cover*
9. White Birch
10. Ground Cover*
11. Knap Hill Azalea
12. White Rhododendron
13. Knap Hill Azalea
14. White Rhododendron
15. Knap Hill Azalea
16. Knap Hill Azalea

*Ground Covers:
   Lamb's Ears
   Lily-of-the-Valley
   Variegated Hostas
   Variegated Pachysandra

Designed by
Betty Pruehsner

Crescent Moon Garden

1. Lamb's Ears
2. Evening Primrose
3. Evening Primrose
4. Sasa Veitchii Bamboo

5. Dwarf Conifer
6. Moonflower (trellised)
7. Daylily

Designed by Cathy Wilkinson Barash

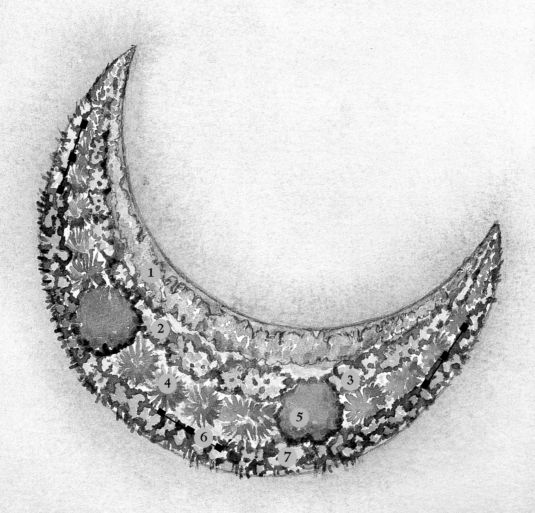

Cathy's Corner

1. Canna
2. Witch Hazel
3. Honeysuckle
4. Cleome 'Helen Campbell'
5. Chamomile
6. English Daisy
7. Pansy 'Antique Shades'
8. White Dahlia
9. Dusty Miller
10. Summer Hyacinth
11. Sweet Alyssum
12. Flowering Tobacco 'Domino Pink'
13. Calla Lily
14. Dusty Miller
15. White Dahlia
16. Moonflower Vine (trained on stakes between windows)
17. Flowering Tobacco
18. Calla Lily
19. Dusty Miller
20. Tuberose
21. Nicotiana Sylvestris
22. Sweet Alyssum
23. White Dahlia
24. Dusty Miller
25. Flowering Tobacco 'Domino Pink'
26. Calla Lily
27. Sweet Alyssum
28. Dusty Miller
29. Moonflower Vine

Designed by Cathy Wilkinson Barash

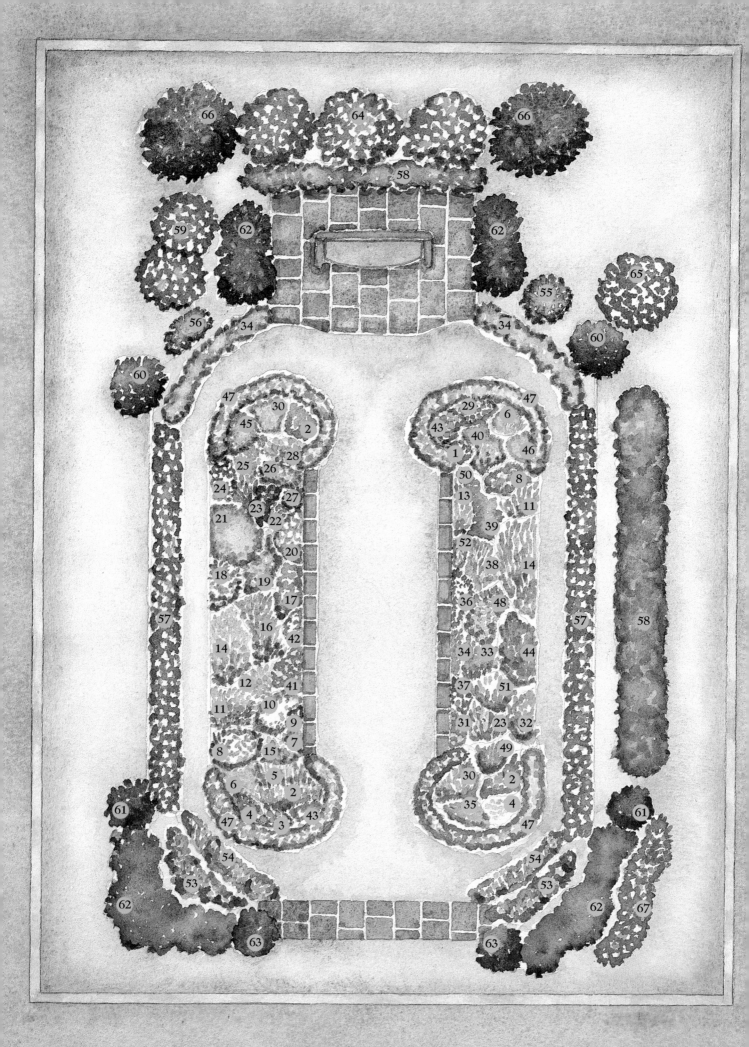

Grey Garden

OLD WESTBURY GARDENS

1. Fan Columbine
2. Woolly Speedwell
3. Stonecrop
4. Allwood Pinks 'Aqua'
5. Wormwood 'Silver Frost'
6. Rue 'Blue Curl'
7. Orostachys
8. Silver Sage
9. Woolly Yarrow
10. Baby's Breath
11. Catmint 'Six Hills Giant'
12. Toadflax 'Canon J. Went'
13. Bugleweed 'SilverBeauty'
14. White Sage 'Silver Queen'
15. Chilean Sorrel
16. Amethyst Sea Holly
17. Apennine Sun Rose
18. Scotch Thistle
19. Blue Fescue
20. Stonecrop 'Vera Jameson'
21. Wormwood 'Powis Castle'
22. Society Garlic
23. Mullein
24. Yarrow
25. Lavender
26. Lamb's Ears 'Silver Carpet'
27. Wall Rock-cress 'Snow Cap'
28. Bethlehem Sage 'Roy Davidson'
29. Allwood Pinks 'Garnet Star'
30. Ornamental Onion
31. Stonecrop 'Rosy Glow'
32. Russian Sage
33. Fringed Lavender
34. Lamb's Ears

35. Myrtle Euphorbia
36. Snow-in-Summer 'Columnae'
37. Canary Clover
38. Blue Oat Grass
39. Woolly Speedwell 'Minuet"
40. Wormwood 'Valerie Finnis'
41. Beach Wormwood 'Silver Brocade'
42. Common Pussytoes
43. Rose Campion 'Oculata'
44. Rattlesnake Master
45. Horehound
46. Blue Cupid's Dart
47. Lavender Cotton
48. Jerusalem Sage
49. Ballota
50. Stonecrop 'Cape Blanco'
51. Loosestrife
52. Cheddar Pinks
53. Blue Mist
54. Catmint 'Dropmore'
55. Butterfly Bush
56. Butterfly Bush 'Alba'
57. Shrub Rose 'Sea Foam'
58. Hicks Yew
59. Koreanspice Viburnum
60. Meserve Hybrid Holly 'Blue Girl'
61. Meserve Hybrid Holly 'Blue Boy'
62. Boxwood 'Welleri'
63. Japanese Holly 'Helleri'
64. Siebold Viburnum
65. Crabapple
66. American Holly
67. Glossy Abelia

Designed by Pat Slator

Sources & Further Reading

Lighting: U.S.

THE AMERICAN LIGHTING ASSOCIATION will give you general lighting information and the name of the lighting showroom nearest you. Call 800-BRIGHTIDEAS. You can also contact lighting fixture companies directly. They will either send you a catalog or refer you to the nearest dealer.

Intermatic, Inc.
Intermatic Plaza, Spring Grove, IL 60081
(815) 675-2321 Free catalog.

The Toro Co.
P O Box 1071, Maple Plain, MN 55348
(800) 321-8676 Free catalog.

Both of these companies specialize in low-cost, low-voltage outdoor-lighting systems. The kits come with transformer, fixtures, wire and complete instructions.

HADCO
128 Craftway, P O Box 100, Littlestown, PA 17340
(717) 359-7131 Catalog $5.

Nightscaping by Loran Inc.
1705 East Colton Avenue, Redlands CA 92374
(714) 794-2121 Free catalog.

These companies work with and supply lighting designers, and also make their products available to individuals. Both companies deal with low-voltage lighting.

Siemens Solar Industries
P O Box 6032, Camarillo, CA 93011
(800) 233-1106
This is the company for solar-powered lighting. Each year they have more products that are more attractive for the garden. Free catalog.

Liteform Designs
P O Box 3316, Portland, OR 97208-3316
(800) 458-2505 Free catalog.

Progress Lighting
Erie Ave. and G. St., Philadelphia, PA 19134
(215) 289-1200 Free catalog.

Task Lighting Corp.
P O Box 1090, Kearney, NE 68848
(800)445-6404 Free catalog.

Look to these companies for a wide variety of lighting fixtures in a range of materials.

Heritage Lanterns
70-A Main St., Yarmouth, ME 04096
(800) 544-6070 Free catalog.

Idaho Wood Lighting
P O Box 488, Sandpoint, ID 83864
(800) 635-1100 Free catalog.

Santa Fe Lights
Route 10, Box 88-Y, Santa Fe, NM 87501
(505) 471-0076 Free catalog.

These three companies have some of the most unique outdoor lighting fixtures. If you are interested in custom work, check with them.

Plant Material: U.S.

INITIALLY IT IS BEST TO LOOK to your local nurseries and garden centers for plant material. As your tastes become more sophisticated, you may have to look farther afield. The source book I rely on has just been revised. *Andersen Horticultural Library's Source List of Plants and Seeds* is a wealth of information. More than 400 retail and wholesale plant sources in the U.S. and Canada are included. It lists over 47,000 different plants by botanic name (tomato, for example is listed as *Lycopersicon* and each different hybrid name is listed with its source). For those not up on Latin, there is a cross reference of common names in the front of the book. To order the book, send a check for $34.95 to:

Andersen Horticultural Library
Minnesota Landscape Arboretum,
3675 Arboretum Drive, Box 39,
Chanhassen, MN 55317

Another must-have guide to locating plant material is *Taylor's Guide to Specialty Nurseries* by Barbara Barton (Houghton Mifflin Company, 1993). Unlike the previous book, this is not just a listing. It is a chatty introduction to the many plantsmen in America, organized by type of plant. Not all the nurseries included do mail order—sometimes you just have to be lucky enough to live nearby.

GENERAL

Logee's Greenhouses
141 North Street, Danielson, CT 06239
(203) 774-8038
Much of their plant material is not hardy in colder climates, but is good in warm climates outdoors year-round. I have a number of Logee's plants that summer outdoors and winter in a sunny room. Large selection of fragrant plants. Catalog $3.

Wayside Gardens
1 Garden Lane, Hodges, SC 29695-0001
(800) 845-1124
Lots of different plants—some rare, others more common from trees and shrubs to perennials and bulbs. Free catalog.

AZALEAS & RHODODENDRONS

Kelleygreen Rhododendron Nursery
P O Box 62, Drain, OR 97435 (503) 836-2290
Good selection of species rhododendrons and hybrids—more than 1600 listed. Catalog $1.25.

Roslyn Nursery
211 Burrs Lane, Dix Hills, NY 11746
(516) 643-9347
More than 800 rhododendrons and 300 azaleas plus other trees, shrubs and perennials. Many very hardy rhododendrons. Catalog $3.

BAMBOO

IF YOU WANT A TOUCH of bamboo for your evening garden, your best bet is to shop the catalogs. Most small nurseries and garden centers do not even have any bamboo—if they do, it is limited to one or two varieties only.

Bamboo Sourcery
666 Wagnon Road, Sebastopol, CA 95472
(707) 823-5866
Grows more than 250 varieties, 100 offered in catalog. Catalog $2.

Choice Plants
Dept. EG, 9 Bloody Pond Road,
Plymouth, MA 02360 (508) 224-7982
A good source for hardy bamboos—also ornamental grasses and some unusual plants. The

one source I found that not only listed but actually had hakonechloa. Free catalog.

Steve Ray's Bamboo Gardens
909 Seventy-ninth Place South,
Birmingham, AL 35206 (205) 833-3052
His collection includes more than 100 varieties. Catalog $2.

BULBS

B & D Lilies
330 P Street, Port Townsend, WA 98368
(206) 385-1738
The catalog is worth saving for the luscious lily photos. Catalog $3.

The Daffodil Mart
Route 3, Box 794, Gloucester, VA 23061
(804) 693-3966
More than 350 daffodils—also other spring-blooming bulbs. Free catalog.

John Scheepers, Inc.
P O Box 700, Bantam, CT 06750 (203) 567-0838
Top quality bulbs for over 80 years. Free catalog.

Mad River Imports
RR1 Box 1685, Moretown VT, 05660
(802) 496-3004
75 summer-blooming and 200 spring-blooming bulbs. Free catalog.

K. Van Bourgondien & Sons, Inc.
P O Box 1000-EG, Babylon, NY 11702
(516) 669-3500
Two separate catalogs that feature spring-blooming and summer-blooming bulbs. Also some choice perennials and hostas. Free catalog.

Van Dyck's Flower Farm, Inc.
P O Box 430-EG, Brightwaters, NY 11718-0430
(800) 248-2852
Quality bulbs at discount prices—shipped direct from Holland to the customer. Free catalog.

Van Engelen, Inc.
313 Maple Street, Litchfield, CT 06759
(203) 567-5662
If you want great quantities of bulbs, this company offers spring-blooming bulbs by the hundreds at good prices. Free catalog.

CACTUS

Desert Nursery
1301 S. Copper St., Deming, NM 88030
(505) 546-6264
Cold-hardy cactus. Some thrive down to zero degrees F if the weather is dry—wet winters can be their death. Price list free.

Grigsby Cactus Gardens
2326 Bella Vista Drive, Vista, CA 92084
(619) 727-1323
Broad cactus selection. Catalog $2.

Mesa Garden
P O Box 72, Belen NM 87002 (505) 864-3131
For patient gardeners who want to grow cactus from seed—this is the source. Also seed-grown plants. Catalog $1.

Midwest Cactus Sales
P O Box 163, New Melle, MO 63365
(314) 828-538
Specializes in cold-hardy cactus. Catalog $1.

DAYLILIES

DAYLILIES ARE ONE OF the easiest plants to grow, rewarding little effort with a lot of show. Look for daylilies with extended bloom (stay open until midnight) or those that are true night-bloomers. Try to visit one of the nurseries near you for a greater selection.

Alpine Valley Gardens
2627 Calistoga Road, Santa Rosa, CA 95404
(707) 539-1749
An official American Hemerocallis Society Display Garden. Good price range of plants.

Floyd Cove Nursery
725 Longwood-Markham Road, Sanford, FL 32771-8315 (407) 324-9229
Lots of unusual daylilies—some of the newest varieties. Catalog $2.

Seawright Gardens
201 Bedford Road, Carlisle, MA 01741
(508) 369-2172
300 daylilies and over 200 hostas in catalog. Catalog $1.

Valente Gardens
RFD 2, Box 234, East Lebanon, ME 04027
(207) 457-2076
300-400 daylilies in catalog. Catalog $0.52.

FERNS

Foliage Gardens
2003 128th Avenue S.E., Bellevue, WA 98005
(206) 747-2998
More than 100 different ferns, including evergreen ferns and sun-tolerant ferns with silvery foliage. Catalog $2.

Varga's Nursery
2631 Pickertown Road, Warrington, PA 18976
(215) 343-0646
Wholesale and retail of tropical and hardy ferns—more than 250 varieties. Catalog $1.

HERBS

SOME OF THOSE WONDERFUL silver-leafed plants are actually herbs—sage, lavender, lavender cotton. Also garlic chives and lamb's ears—stars of the evening garden.

Edgewood Farm & Nursery
Route 2, Box 303. Stanardsville, VA 22973-9405
(804) 985-3782
More than 500 varieties of herbs—great selection of many varieties. Catalog $2.

Merry Gardens
P O Box 595, Camden, ME 04843
(207) 236-9064
Great selection of over 200 herbs—also 125 different ivies. Catalog $2.

Nichols Garden Nursery, Inc.
1190 N. Pacific Highway, Albany, OR 97321
(503) 928-9280
Herb plants as well as vegetable seeds. Free catalog.

Sandy Mush Herb Nursery
316 Surrett Cove Road, Leicester, NC 28748
(704) 683-2014
Good source for unusual varieties of herbs. Also some perennials. Catalog $4.

Well-Sweep Herb Farm
317 Mt. Bethel Road, Port Murray, NJ 07865
(908) 852-5390
Among the best selections of different varieties of herbs. If you want a collection of lavenders, rosemaries, thymes, etc. this is where to find the plants. Catalog $2.

HOSTAS

Homestead Division of Sunnybrook Farms
9448 Mayfield Road, Chesterland, OH 44026
(216) 729-9838
A leading source of hostas offering more than 200 plants and seeds of about 1,000 hosta varieties. Also daylilies. Catalog $2.

Robyn's Nest Nursery
7802 N.E. Sixty-third Street, Vancouver, WA 98662 (206) 256-7399
200 species and cultivars. Good astilbe selection. Catalog $2.

LILACS

Falcon's Keep Gardens
P O Box 1529, Medina, OH 44258 (216) 723-4966
Offers the hybrids of the late Brother John Fiala, a great hybridizer. Free catalog.

Heard Gardens, Ltd.
5355 Merle Hay Road, Johnston, IA 50131
(515) 276-4533
More than 45 lilacs, listed by flower color. Offers several "low-chill" varieties that bloom in the South. Catalog $2.

Wedge Nursery
Route 2, Box 114, Albert Lea, MN 56007
(507) 373-5225
Family nursery since 1878—50 to 70 varieties offered from propagation of 150 varieties grown. Free catalog.

ORNAMENTAL GRASSES

Greenlee Nursery
301 E. Franklin Avenue, Pomona, CA 91766
(714) 629-9045
Over 150 grasses, especially those suited for
Western gardens. Catalog $5.

Kurt Bluemel, Inc.
2740 Greene Lane, Baldwin, MD 21013-9523
(410) 557-7229
The name that is almost synonymous with
ornamental grasses lists hundreds of different
grasses including many German cultivars.
Catalog $3.

Limerock Ornamental Grasses
RD 1, Box 111C, Port Matilda, PA 16870
(814) 692-2272
More than 100 varieties of grasses, limited numbers
of bamboo and hardy ferns. Catalog $2.

PALMS

IF YOU LIVE IN A CLIMATE WARM enough to grow
palms outdoors, or want to consider them for
indoors, all these nurseries have good selections.

Neon Palm Nursery
3525 Stony Point Road, Santa Rosa, CA 95407
(707) 585-8100
78 species of palms, many cycads, some bamboo
and other plants. Catalog $1.

Pacific Tree Farms
4301 Lynwood Drive, Chula Vista, CA 92010
(619) 422-2400
Palms and a good variety of other subtropical trees.
Catalog $2.

The Green Escape
P O Box 1417, Palm Harbor, FL 34682-1417
(813) 784-1991
More than 300 palms available by mail order.
Catalog $6.

PERENNIALS

Bluestone Perennials
7211 Middle Ridge Road, Madison, OH 44057
(800) 852-5243
500 perennials for the gardener on a budget—small
plants at low prices. You just have to have patience
for them to grow into their full size. Free catalog.

Busse Gardens
13579 10th Street NW, Cokato, MN 55321
(612) 286-2654
Look here for perennials you can't find elsewhere—
also cold-hardy plants. Catalog $2.

Donaroma's Nursery
P O Box 2189, Edgartown, MA 02539
(508) 627-8366
Offers over 450 perennials—most summer
bloomers. Free catalog.

Milaeger's Gardens
4838 Douglas Avenue, Racine WI 53402-2498
(414) 639-2371
Prodigious number of plants offered in their
"Perennial Wishbook." Catalog $1.

Niche Gardens
111 Dawson Road, Chapel Hill, NC 27516
(919) 967-0078
A good number of unusual perennials as well as
native plants and plants for specific requirements
(drought-tolerant, bog, shade). Catalog $3.

White Flower Farm
Route 63, Litchfield, CT 06759-0050
(203)496-9624
Their catalog should be saved as a plant reference.
Wide range of perennials plus bulbs, shrubs and
vines. Catalog $5.

TREES AND SHRUBS

Coenosium Gardens
P O Box 847, Sandy, OR 97055
(503) 668-3574
Offer more than 600 different cultivars of dwarf
conifers. Catalog $3.

Forestfarm
990 Tetherow Road, Williams, OR 97544-9599
(503) 846-7269
Good selection of trees, shrubs, and perennials at
low prices. The plants are very small, so it will take
time for them to fill in the garden, but worth the
wait in economic savings. Catalog $3.

Gossler Farms Nursery
1200 Weaver Road, Springfield, OR 97478-9663
(503) 746-3922
Lovely choices of plants that provide interest in the
garden in autumn, winter and early spring.
Catalog $2.

Lamtree Farm
Route 1, Box 162, Warrensville, SC 28693
(919) 385-6144
Specialize in native trees and shrubs of the
Southeast. Catalog $2.

Mellinger's
2310 W. South Range Road,
North Lima, OH 44452 (216) 549-9861
Excellent selection of trees. Free catalog.

Musser Forests, Inc.
P O Box 340, Indiana, PA 15701 (412) 465-5686
Trees and shrubs in seedling sizes. Good source for
quantities of trees at reasonable prices—patience
required for them to grow. Free catalog.

Rarafolia
16 Beverly Drive, Kintnersville, PA 18930
(215) 847-8208
Offers over 400 dwarf conifers. Also more than 100
different Japanese maples. Catalog $3.

Woodlanders, Inc.
1128 Colleton Avenue, Aiken, SC 29801
(803) 648-7522
Great source for plants for hardiness Zone 8 and above. Catalog $2.

Yucca Do Nursery
P O Box 655, Waller, TX 77484 (409) 826-6363
Trees, shrubs and more, especially suited for the Southwest. Catalog $3.

WATER LILIES

Tilley's Nursery/The WaterWorks
111 E. Fairmount St., Coopersburg, PA 18036
(215) 282-4784
Water lilies, lotus, supplies and fish. Catalog $3.

Lilypons Water Gardens
6800 Lilypons Road, P O Box 10,
Buckeystown, MD 21717-0010 (301) 874-5133
All you need to make a water garden from pond liners to plants. Free catalog.

Van Ness Water Gardens
2460 N. Euclid Ave., Upland, CA 91784
(714) 982-2425
Good selection of plants and water gardening supplies. Catalog $2.

SEEDS

IF YOU ARE A BIT MORE AMBITIOUS, you may want to try growing plants from seed. There is a greater selection of annuals and vegetables if you shop the seed catalogs rather than buying the six-packs at a local nursery or garden center.

Johnny's Selected Seeds
Foss Hill Road, Box 2580, Albion, ME 04910
(207) 437-9294
Offers a full range of vegetable seeds, with emphasis on those that will thrive in cool climates. Free catalog.

Park Seed Co.
P O Box 31, Greenwood, SC 29648
(803) 223-8555
A big seed company that has been around for more than 100 years. They offer a broad range of annuals, perennials and vegetables. Free catalog.

Seeds Blum
Idaho City Stage, Boise, ID 83706
(208) 342-0858
A small seed company that specializes in heirloom varieties of vegetables and ornamentals. Try white eggplant or white tomatoes for a highlight in the evening garden. Catalog $3.

Shepherd's Garden Seeds
6116 Highway 9, Felton, CA 95018 (408) 335-5400
30 Irene Street, Torrington, CT 06790
(203) 482-3638
A wonderful collection of seeds—edibles and ornamentals. Many European varieties. Catalog $1.

Thompson & Morgan Seed Co.
Box 1308, Jackson, NJ 08527 (908) 363-2225
A British seed company with a huge range of seeds—annuals, perennials, some trees, fruits and vegetables. Free catalog.

W. Atlee Burpee Co.
300 Park Avenue, Warminster, PA. 18974
(215) 674-4900
Another one of the American giants in the seed industry. They offer a broad range of seed from annuals, perennials, fruits and vegetables. Also some plants and bulbs. Free catalog.

Lighting: Canada

SOME GARDEN SUPPLY CENTERS and large lighting equipment dealers offer supplies and advice, as will some of the companies listed for the U. S. Call 1-800 BRIGHTIDEAS in some parts of Canada.

Heritage Casting and Ironworks, Ltd.
250 Trowers Road, Unit 4,
Woodbridge, ON L4L 5Z6 (416) 856-2508
Victorian garden lighting and other equipment. Free catalog.

Plant Material: Canada

SOME OF THE U.S. companies listed previously will ship to Canada, especially if the order is large. In order to import plant materials—including roots, bulbs, corms, etc.—the buyer must obtain an import permit, obtainable free of charge from:

Plant Protection Division, Agriculture Canada, Ottawa, Ontario K1A 0C6

Most seeds can be imported without a permit.

Brackenstone Herbs
Box 752, Nelson, BC V1L 5R7
Herb plants and seeds. Catalog $3.

Corn Hill Nursery, Ltd.
RR5, Petitcodiac, NB E0A 2H0 (506) 756-3635
Trees, shrubs, lilacs, perennials. Catalog $2.

Ferncliff Gardens
8394 McTaggart Street, Mission, BC V2V 6S6
(604) 826-2447
Day lilies, gladiolus, peonies, iris. Catalog $2.

Gardenimport, Inc.
P O Box 760, Thornhill, ON L3T 4A5
(800) 565-0957 or (416) 731-1950
Imported seeds, bulbs, ferns, perennials. Catalog subscription $4.

McConnell's Nurseries, Inc.
Port Burwell, ON N0J 1T0 (519) 874-4800
Seeds, shrubs, trees. Free catalog.

Monashee Perennials
RR7 Site 6, Box 9, Vernon, BC V1T 7Z3
(604) 542-2592
Day lilies, hosta, perennials. Catalog $2.

Moore Water Gardens
P.O. Box 70 Hwy 4, Port Stanley, ON N5L 1J4
(519) 782-4052 Free catalog.

Picov's Greenhouses
380 Kingston Rd. East, Ajax, ON L1S 4S7
(416) 686-2151
Water gardening and perennials; hardy bamboo;
dwarf conifers and trees. Free catalogs.

Prism Perennials
C45, S25 RR1, Castlegar, BC V1N 3H7
(604) 365-3753
Perennials, day lilies, ornamental grasses, herbs.
Catalog $2.

Reimer Waterscapes
Box 34, Tillsonburg, ON N4G 4H3
(519) 842-6049 Free catalog.

Richter's Herbs
357 Highway 57, Goodwood, ON L0C 1A0
(416) 640-6677
Herb seeds, plants. Catalog $2.

Further Reading

My personal gardening library has nearly a
thousand books—many of which I referred to in
writing this book. The following are the ones I
found myself drawn to the most.

Western Garden Book
Sunset Magazine Book editors
Sunset Publishing, 1988
Hardcover: $24.95; Paperback: $18.95
This is my reference for gardening in the West and
Southwest. It gives good general gardening
information, followed by an extensive listing of
plants.

Fragrant Flowers
Denise Greig
Kangaroo Press Pty Ltd, 1990, Paperback: $12.95
A small book with an Australian accent. A few of
the plants listed may be obscure to Eastern gardeners,
but more readily available on the West Coast.

Daylilies: The Perfect Perennial
Lewis & Nancy Hill
Storey Communications, Inc., 1991
Hardcover: $24.95; Paperback: $14.95
Everything you wanted to know about daylilies
from A to Z in a concise, easy-to-read form.

**The Adventurous Gardener's Sourcebook of Rare
and Unusual Plants**
William C. Mulligan
Simon & Schuster, 1993, Hardcover: $40.00
This book is perfect for the intermediate to
advanced gardener who has become bored with
seeing and growing the same old plant material
year after year.

Ornamental Grasses—The Amber Wave
Carole Ottesen
McGraw-Hill Publishing Company, 1989
Hardcover: $29.95
Covers ornamental grasses, sedges, reeds, bamboos
and grasslike plants. It shows the complete range of
plants—with sizes, shapes and colors to suit any
garden.

Bamboos
Christine Recht & Max F. Wetterwald
Timber Press, 1992. Hardcover: $32.95
There seems to be a paucity of written material on
bamboos—this book is a translation from the
original German. It is up to date with name
changes and good descriptions of the plants.

Growing Fragrant Plants
Rayford Clayton Reddell & Robert Galyean
Harper & Row, Publishers, 1989.
Hardcover: $35.95
For cultural information, this is the best book of
fragrant plants. It gives a broad range of cultivars
and species and a lot of useful information.

The Scented Garden
Rosemary Verey
Random House, 1981. Hardcover: $24.95
Verey has a lovely, chatty style of writing. The book
is divided into six plant sections—roses; annuals,
biennials and perennials; bulbs, corms and tubers;
herbs; shrubs, trees and climbers; and fragrant
exotica.

Taylor's Guide to Annuals
Norman Taylor
Houghton Mifflin Company, 1986
Paperback: $16.95 (Revised Edition)

Taylor's Guide to Shrubs
Norman Taylor
Houghton Mifflin Company, 1987
Paperback: $16.95

Taylor's Guide to Bulbs
Norman Taylor
Houghton Mifflin Company, 1987
Paperback: $16.95

All of the Taylor Guides are excellent sources of
information. Good photographs grouped by color
of the flowers or foliage.

Hardiness Zone Map

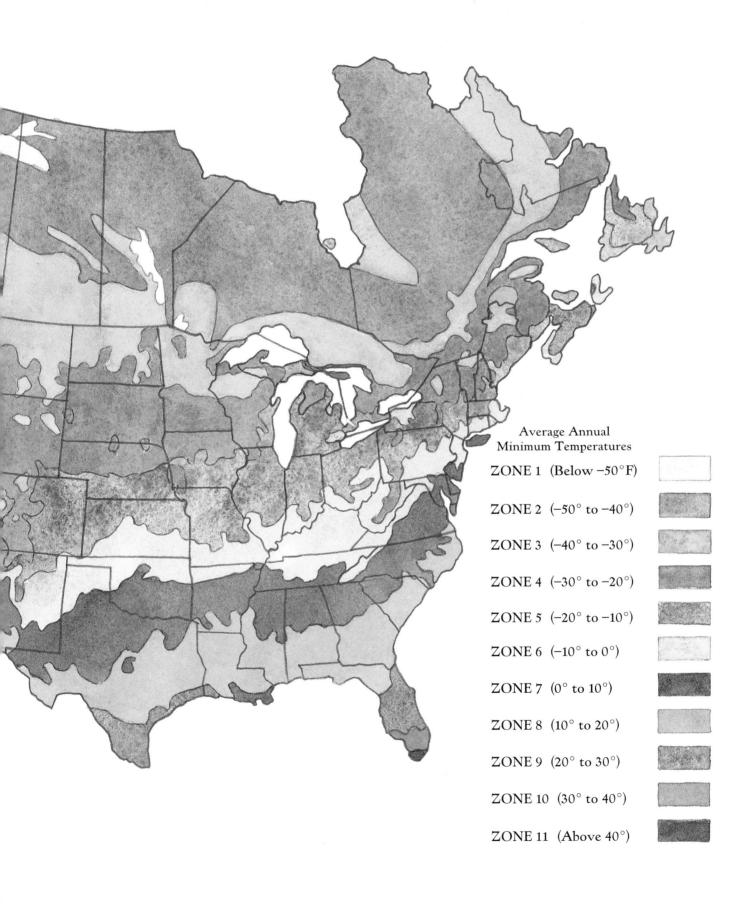

Average Annual
Minimum Temperatures

ZONE 1 (Below −50°F)

ZONE 2 (−50° to −40°)

ZONE 3 (−40° to −30°)

ZONE 4 (−30° to −20°)

ZONE 5 (−20° to −10°)

ZONE 6 (−10° to 0°)

ZONE 7 (0° to 10°)

ZONE 8 (10° to 20°)

ZONE 9 (20° to 30°)

ZONE 10 (30° to 40°)

ZONE 11 (Above 40°)

Photography Credits

Calla lilies' beauty and grace is unmatched in the evening garden.

CATHY WILKINSON BARASH

Pages: 2, 8-9, 10, 11, 12, 15, 16, 17, 19 (top right), 22, 24, 25, 26, 35, 37, 38, 40, 41, 42 (top left), 44, 45, 46, 48, 52 (top left), 54, 58, 60, 61, 63, 64, 65, 68, 69, 70 (top and bottom), 72, 74, 77, 78 (top and bottom), 79, 80, 83, 84 (left), 85, 86, 87, 91 (top), 102, 104 (left), 108, 111, 112, 114 (top and bottom), 118, 120, 124 (top), 129, 133, 135 (right), 137 (top), 141, 142, 144, 145 (bottom), 146, 147, 153 (top and bottom), 154, 156, 157, back cover

DEREK FELL

Pages: Cover, 4-5, 6-7, 13, 14, 18-19, 20, 21, 23, 27, 29, 31, 32, 33, 36, 42-43, 47, 49, 50, 51, 52-53, 55, 56, 57, 59, 62, 66, 67, 71, 73, 75, 76, 81, 82, 84 (right), 88 (top left), 88-89, 90, 91 (bottom), 92-93, 94, 95, 97, 98, 99, 100, 101, 103, 104-105, 106, 109, 110, 113, 115, 116, 117, 119, 121, 122, 123, 124 (bottom), 125, 126, 127, 128, 130, 131, 132, 134-135, 137 (bottom), 138, 139, 140, 143, 145 (top), 152, 172

Turid Forsyth: Pages 30 and 136; Susanne Lucas: Page 39; John Minet: Page 107; Carol Ottesen: Page 28; John N. Trager: Pages 34 and 96.
Courtesy of Butchart Gardens: Page 155
Courtesy of HADCO: Pages 148 and 150
Courtesy of Intermatic: Page 153 (bottom)
Courtesy of Nightscaping: Pages 149 and 151

Index

Acer
    griseum, 58; photo, 56
    palmatum, photo, 52-53
    palmatum 'Dissectum,' 53-54
    pensylvanicum, 56-58
Acorus gramineus 'Variegatus,' 52
Adam's needle, 51-52; photo, 51
Adiantum pedatum, 45
Aegopodium podagraria 'Variegatum,' 114
Ageratum, 81
Allium tuberosum, 133-135; photo, 134-135
Alyssum, 17, 20, 81, 88-89
Amberboa moschata ssp. suaveolens, 69-70
Andromeda, 82
Anemone, Japanese, 21
Angel's trumpet (*Brugmansia*), 96; photos, 5, 94, 95
Angel's trumpet (*Datura*), 136-137; photos, 30, 136
Arbors, 25-26
Arbutus unedo, 44
Architectural elements of the garden, 18-19, 23-29
Architectural plants, 21, 36-55
Artemisia, 24
    schmidtiana 'Silver Mound,' 108-109
Artichoke, 135-136; photo, 135
Arum italicum 'Pictum,' 114; photo, 114
Aruncus dioicus, 82; photo, 82
Arundinaria auricoma, 40
Aster, 35
Athyrium goeringianum 'Pictum'
Athyrium nipponicum 'Pictum,' 115; photo, 114
Azaleas
    Exbury hybrid, 70; photo, 70. See also *Rhododendron*
    Knap Hill, 70
Baby's breath, 87
Bamboos, 19, 37-40; photos, 37, 38, 39
    black, 39-40; photo, 39
    clumping, 38, 39
    cultivation, 38-39
    fountain, 39
    hardiness, 37-38
    henon, 40
    kumazasa, 40; photo, 40
    running, 38, 39-40
    umbrella, 38, 39
    whitestripe, dwarf, 120
Bark, textured, 56-59
Basket-flower, 87; photo, 14
Basswood, 131-132; photo, 131
Bee balm, 66
Bellflower, peach-leaved, 61-62; photo, 62
Bergamot, 66
Betula
    nigra, 58-59; photo, 59
    papyrifera, 58; photo, 57

Birch
    canoe, 24, 58
    paper, 56; photo, 57
    red, 58-59
    river, 58-59; photo, 59
Bishop's weed, variegated, 114
Black snakeroot, 82
Black-eyed susan, 17
Black-eyed susan vine, 69
Bleeding heart, white, 82
Blood grass, Japanese, 64
Bloodroot, 82
Blue star creeper, 78-79; photo, 78
Boltonia, 35
Brassica oleracea, Acephala Group, 115-116; photo, 115
Bricks in paths, 28
Bridalwreath, 90-91; photo, 90
Bright flowers, 69-76
Brugmansia, photos, 5, 94, 95
    'Betty Marshall,' 96
    'Charles Grimaldi,' 96
    sanguinea, 96
    suaveolens, 96
Bugbane, Kamchatka, 82
Cabbage, flowering, 115-116
Cacti, 33, 40-42, 96. See also Cereus.
    cultivation, 41
    epiphyllum, 98
    golden barrel, 41
    monvillea, 102
    old man, 97
    organ-pipe, 101-102
    prickly pear, 40, 42; photo, 42
    saguaro, 36, 96, 97; photo, 96
Caladium x *hortulanum*, 116-118; photo, 116
    'Candidum,' 116; photo, 113
    'Frieda Hemple,' 116
    'White Queen,' 116
Calamint, 77-78; photo, 78
Calamintha
    nepeta nepeta, 77-78; photo, 78
    nepetoides, 77-78; photo, 78
Calendula, 32
Calla lily, 91-93; photos, 11, 91, 92-93
Campanula, 77
    persicifolia, 61-62; photo, 62
Candytuft, 17, 87-88; photo, 88
Canna x *generalis*, 70-71; photo, 70
    'City of Portland,' 70
    'Pfitzer's Primrose Yellow,' 70
    'Richard Wallace,' 70
    'Wyoming,' 70
Cardinal flower, 17, 31, 64-66
Cardoon, 109; photo, 109
Carnegiea gigantea, 97; photo, 96
Carob, 44
Cathy's corner garden plan, 161
Cedar, 44
Centaurea
    maritima, 112

    moschata ssp. suaveolens, 69-70
Cephalocereus senilis, 97
Cerastium tomentosum, 82
Ceratonia siliqua, 44
Cereus, 96; photos, 17, 101
    dayamii, photo, 17
    night-blooming (*Cereus*), 135; photo, 133
    night-blooming (*Hylocereus*), 101; photo, 100
    night-blooming (*Nyctocereus*), 102-103; photo, 102
    night-blooming (*Selenicereus*), 106-107; photos, 106, 107
    peruvianus, 135; photo, 133
    serpentinus, 103
Cestrum nocturnum, 97-98; photo, 97
Chamaecyparis obtusa 'Crippsii,' 45
Chamaerops excelsa, 50
Checkered lily, 85; photo, 85
Chelone lyonii, 62-63
Chinese chive, 133-135; photo, 134-135
Chionodoxa luciliae, 62; photo, 61
Chive, garlic, 133-135; photo, 134-135
Chrysanthemum, 21
Cimicifuga
    racemosa, 82
    simplex, 82
Cineraria, 17, 63; photo, 63
    maritima, 112
Citrus
    limon, 124-125; photo, 124
    sinensis, 124-125; photo, 124
Citrus trees, dwarf, 42
Clematis, 24, 26, 32, 64; photos, 31, 64, 65
    autumn, 17, 64
    'Duchess of Edinburgh,' 64
    'Ernest Markham,' 32
    'Henryi,' 64
    x *jackmanii*, 19, 32, 64
    maximowicziana, 64
    'Nelly Moser,' 64
    'Ville de Lyon,' 64
Cleome, 20
Climatic zones, map, 170-171
Coffea arabica, 123-124
Coffee, 123-124
Coleus x *hybridus*, 64
    'Bellingrath Pink,' 64
    'Fashion Parade' series, 64
Color in the evening garden, 23, 31-33, 69
Concrete in paths, 28
Coneflower, orange, 73; photo, 73
Conifers, dwarf, 20
Contour lighting, 151
Contrasting foliage plants, 113-121
Coreopsis verticillata 'Moonbeam,' 32, 71; photo, 71
Cornus
    alba, 59; photo, 58
    contraversa 'Variegata,' 114
    sericea 'Flaviramea,' 59
    stolonifera 'Flaviramea,' 59

Cortaderia selloana, 47-48; photo, 47
Corylus avellana 'Contorta,' 55; photo, 54.
  See also Harry Lauder's walking stick
Cosmos, 33, 81
Cotoneaster horizontalis, 54-55
Cowslip, 32
Crescent moon garden plan, 160
Crocus, 19, 33
Crosslighting, 151
Cupflower, 90 *Nierembergia* 'Mont Blanc'
x *Cupressocyparis leylandii* 'Silverdust,' 45
Cycad, 50-51, 127
Cycas revoluta, 50-51
Cynara
  cardunculus, 109; photo, 109
  scolymus 135-136; photo, 135
Cypress
  hinoki false, 45
  leyland, 'Silverdust,' 45
Daffodils, 62, 72-73; photos, 21, 68.
  See also *Narcissus*
  Peruvian, 87; photos, 14, 87
Dahlia, 21, 82, 138
Daisy, gloriosa, 69
Daphne
  x *burkwoodii* 'Carol Mackie,' 137;
    photo, 137
  cneorum, 79; photo, 77
Date palm, pygmy, 49-50
Datura, 19, 96; photo, 30
  'Evening Fragrance,' 136-137
  inoxia, 136-137; photo, 136
  meteloides, 136-137; photo, 136
Davidia involucrata, 82-83; photo, 83
Daylily, 77, 98-101; photos, 2, 98, 99
Design, lighting, 148-150
Dodecatheon meadia, 83
Dogwood, 82, 113-114
  red-barked, 59; photo, 58
  tatarian, 59
  yellow-twig, 59
Doronicum cordatum, 71
Dove tree, 82-83; photo, 83
Downlighting, 151
Dusty miller, 33, 46, 112; photo, 108
Echinocactus grusonii, 41
Epiphyllum
  crenatum 'Chichicastenango,' photo, 34
  oxypetalum, 98
Erica
  carnea, 84
  herbacea, 84; photo, 84
Eucalyptus, 44; photo, 44
Euphorbia marginata, 137-138; photo, 137
Evening primrose, 77, 104-106; photos,
  35, 104, 105. See also *Oenothera*
Evergreens, 37, 42-45
  dwarf, 42-43
  for impact, 44
  variegated, 45
  with flowers, 44-45
Exbury hybrid azaleas, 70; photo, 70

Fargesia
  murielae, 39
  nitida, 39
Feijoa sellowiana, 44
Fences, 24-25
Fennel, 52-53; photo, 52
Ferns, 45-46, 127
  Christmas, 46; photo, 46
  cinnamon, 45-46; photo, 45
  five-finger, 45
  Japanese-painted, 115; photo, 114
  maidenhair, 45
  royal, 46
Fescue, blue, 46, 48
Festuca ovina glauca, 48
Feverfew, 82
Five spot, 79-80; photo, 79
Fixtures, lighting, 153-154
Floodlights, 153-154; photo, 153
Flowering tobacco, See *Nicotiana*;
  Tobacco, flowering
Foeniculum vulgare, 52-53; photo, 52
Foliage plants. See also Evergreens
  contrasting, 113-121
  silver, 24, 108-112
  variegated, 19, 32, 45, 113-121
Forget-me-nots, photo, 60
Fothergilla gardenii, 84-85; photo, 84
Four o'clock, 19, 103-104; photo, 103
Fragrant plants, 33, 35, 122-132
Franklinia, 35
Fritillaria meleagris, 85; photo, 85
Funkia, 140-141. See also *Hosta*
Galanthus nivalis, 85; photo, 81.
  See also Snowdrop
Galium odoratum, 86
Galtonia candicans, 138; photo, 138.
  See also Hyacinth, summer
Garden plans, 157-162
Gardener's garters, 119-120; photos,
  6, 119
Gardenia jasminoides, 125-126; photos,
  122, 125
  'August Beauty,' 125
  'Golden Magic,' 125-126
  'Mystery,' 126
  'Radicans,' 126
  'Veitchii,' 126
Garlic chive, 133-135; photo, 134-135
Gates, 25
Gaura lindheimeri, 86-87; photo, 86
Gazebos, 26
Geranium, 31
Ghostweed, 137-138; photo, 137
Ginger, kahili, 127; photo, 127
Gladiolus tristis, 126-127; photo, 126
Gloriosa daisy, 69
Glory-of-the-snow, 62; photo, 61
Goatsbeard, 82; photo, 82
Gold hakonechloa, 118; photo, 117
Goldenrod, 69
Goutweed, 114

Grape hyacinth, 66
Grasses, ornamental, 37, 46-49; photos,
  36, 47, 48
Gravel in paths, 28
Gray garden plan, 162
Grazing, 150
Ground pink, 80; photo, 80
Guava, pineapple, 42, 44
Guinea-hen flower, 85; photo, 85
Gypsophila paniculata, 87
Hakonechloa macra aureola, 118; photo, 117
Handkerchief tree, 82-83; photo, 83
Hardscape, 18-19, 23-29
Harry Lauder's walking stick, 33, 55;
  photo, 54
Heather, winter-flowering, 84
Hedera, 113
Hedychium gardneranum, 127; photo, 127
Heliotrope, 20, 138; photos, 23, 139
Heliotropium arborescens, 138-140;
  photo, 139
Hemerocallis, 98-101; photos, 2, 98, 99
  'After the Fall,' 99
  'Beauty to Behold,' 99
  'Bitsy,' 99
  'Blossom Valley,' 99
  'Border Giant,' 99
  'Chorus Line,' 99
  'Cosmic Hummingbird,' 99
  'Diamond Anniversary,' 99
  'Evening Bell,' 99-100
  fulva, 99
  'Gloria Blanca,' 100
  'Goddess,' photo, 2
  'Hudson Valley,' 100
  'Hyperion,' photo, 98
  'Pat Mercer,' 99
  'Paul Bunyan,' 100
Hemlock, 32; photo, 43
  white-tipped, 19
Herbs, 35
Herringbone cotoneaster, 54-55
High-pressure sodium lamps, 153
Holly, 32, 37, 42
  Meserve, 42
  variegated, 45
Holly olive, 130-131
Holly osmanthus, 130-131
Honeysuckle, 24, 25, 129; photo, 129
Hosta, 32, 35, 140-141; photo, 140
  plantaginea 'Aphrodite,' 141
  'Sum and Substance,' 140-141
  'Thumb Nail,' 140
Hyacinth
  grape, 66
  summer, 20, 138; photo, 138
  wood, photo, 60
Hydrangea, 82
Hylocereus undatus, 98, 101; photo, 100
Hymenocallis narcissiflora, 87; photos, 14,
  87
Hymenosporum flavum, 45

Iberis sempervirens, 87-88; photo, 88.
  See also Candytuft
Ilex meserveae, 42
Impatiens, 81
  New Guinea, 35
Imperata cylindrica 'Red Baron,' 64
Ipomoea alba, 141-142; photo, 10, 141.
  See also Moonflower
Ismene calathina, 87
Isotoma fluviatilis, 17, 78-79
Italian arum, variegated, 114; photo, 114
Itea virginica, 88
Ivy, variegated, 32, 113
Jasmine, 26
  Arabian, 127-128
  cape, 125-126
Jasminum sambac, 127-128
  'Maid of Orleans,' 128
Jessamine, night-flowering, 97-98;
  photo, 97
Juniper, 43
  'Bar Harbor,' 42
  'Glauca,' 43
Juniperus horizontalis, 43
Kahili ginger, 127; photo, 127
Kale, flowering, 115-116; photo, 115
Kniphofia uvaria, 71-72; photo, 72
Kohlrabi, 35
Kumazasa, 40; photo, 40. See also
  Sasa veitchii
Lamb's ears, 145; photo, 145
Lamiastrum galeobdolon, 118; photo, 118
  'Herman's Pride,' 118
  'Variegatum,' 118
Lamp types, 152-153
Lathyrus odoratus, 128-129; photo, 128
Laurentia fluviatilis, 78-79; photo, 78
Lavandula, 109-110; photos, 110, 111
  angustifolia, 110
  officinalis, 110
  spica, 110
  stoechas, 110
  vera, 109-110
Lavender, 109-110; photos, 110, 111
Lavender cotton, 20, 111; photo, 111
Lemaireocereus thurberi, 101-102
Lemon, 124-125; photo, 124
Leopard's bane, 71
Lighting, 19-20, 147-155
  automatic control of, 155
  bulbs, 152-153
  design, 148-150
  fixtures, 153-154
  gazebos, 26
  low-voltage, 148
  ornaments, 29
  paths, 28
  techniques, 150-152
  trees, 56
  water, 28-29, 154
Lilac, 123, 131
Lily-of-the-valley, 82

Lilyturf, 19, 113
Lime tree, 131-132; photo, 131
Limonium sinuatum, 72
Linden, 131-132; photo, 131
Liriope, 113. See also Lilyturf
Lobelia cardinalis, 64-66
Lobularia maritima, 88-89. See also
  Alyssum
Lonicera, photo, 129
  fragrantissima, 129
  japonica, 129
Loosestrife, gooseneck, 82, 89-90;
  photo, 88-89
Low-growing pale flowers, 77-80
Luminarias, 154; photo, 149
Lungwort, 120; photos, 120, 121
Lysimachia clethroides, 89-90; photo, 88-89.
  See also Loosestrife, gooseneck
Magnolia, 82
  grandiflora, 44; photo, 20
Maiden grass, 48-49
Maple
  Japanese, 21, 33; photo, 52-53
  Japanese, cut-leaf, 53-54
  paperbark, 58; photo, 56
  snake-bark, 35, 58
  striped, 56-58
Marigold, 32, 74; photos, 69, 74
Marvel of Peru, 103-104; photo, 103
Matthiola
  bicornis, 142-143
  incana, 142; photos, 19, 142
Mercury vapor lamps, 153
Mignonette, 122, 131
Mirabilis jalapa, 103-104; photo, 103.
  See also Four o'clock
Mirroring, 150
Miscanthus sinensis, 47, 48-49
Missouri primrose, 104
Monarda
  didyma, 66
  fistulosa, 66
Monvillea, 101, 102
  cavendishii, 102
  phatnosperma, 102
  spegazzinii, 102
Moon cereus, 106-107; photos, 106, 107
Moonflower, 19, 21, 24, 25, 26, 33, 81, 96,
  122, 123, 141-142; photos, 10, 141
Moonlighting, 151; photo, 148
Moosewood, 56-58
Moss pink, 80; photo, 80
Muscari armeniacum, 66
Narcissus, 72-73; photos, 21, 68
  asturiensis, 72
  'Cassata,' 73
  paper-white, 123
  poeticus, 72
Narrow-leaf yucca, 51
Nasturtium, 69
Nemophila maculata 'Five Spot,' 79-80;
  photo, 79

Nerium oleander, 129-130; photos, 32, 130
Nicotiana, 19, 123. See also Tobacco,
  flowering
  alata, 143; photo, 123
  sylvestris, 143; photo, 143
Nierembergia 'Mont Blanc,' 90
Night-blooming flowers, 33, 94-107
Nycterinia capensis 107
Nyctocereus, 101, 102-103; photo, 102
  guatemalensis, 102-103
  hirschtianus, 103
  serpentinus, 103
Nymphaea, 144; photo, 144
  'Albert Greenberg,' photo, 16
Oenothera, 104-106; photo, 105
  acaulis, 104-105
  argillicola, 105
  biennis, 104
  caespitosa, 106
  californica, 106
  erutheosa 'Sundrop,' photo, 35
  erythrosepala, 106
  fruticosa, 104
  macrocarpa, 104
  missourensis, 104
  speciosa, photo, 104
  taraxacifolia, 104-105
Old man cactus, 97
Oleander, 129-130; photos, 32, 130
Olive, sweet, 20
Opuntia, 42; photo, 42
  humifusa, 40
Orange, 124-125; photo, 124
Orange coneflower, 73
Organ-pipe cactus, 101-102
Ornaments, 29
Osmanthus, 42
  heterophyllus, 130-131
  cinnamomea, 45-46; photo, 45
  regalis, 46 ferns, royal
Oswego tea, 66
Painted fern, Japanese, 115; photo, 114
Pale-colored flowers, 77-80
Palm trees, 36, 49-50, 127
  chusan, 50
  desert fan, 50; photo, 50
  pygmy date, 49-50; photo, 49
  sago palm, 50-51
  windmill, 50
Palmella, 51
Pampas grass, 47-48; photo, 47
Pancratium calathinum, 87
Papaver rhoeas, 67; photos, 12, 67
Pat Lanza garden plan, 158
Paths, 26-28
  lighting, 151-152
Pergolas, 25-26
Perovskia atriplicifolia, 110; photo, 110
Perspective lighting, 150
Peruvian daffodil, 87; photos, 14, 87
Petunia x *hybrida*, 66-67, 77; photo, 66
Phalaris arundinacea picta, 119-120;

photos, 6, 119
Pheasant's eye, 72
Phlox, 82
    night, 107
    subulata, 80; photo, 80
Phoenix roebelenii, 49-50; photo, 49
Phyllostachys nigra, 39-40; photo, 39
    'Henon,' 40
Picea pungens glauca, 45
Pine, dwarf red, 43
Plantain lily, 140-141. See also *Hosta*
Pleioblastus
    variegatus, 120
    viridistratus, 40
Poet's narcissus, 72
Polianthes tuberosa, 144-145; photo, 145.
  See also Tuberose
Polystichum acrostichoides, 46; photo, 46
Poppy, Shirley, 67; photos, 12, 67
Porcupine grass, 33, 49
Prickly pear, 40; photo, 42
Primrose, evening, 77, 104-106; photos,
  35, 104, 105. See also *Oenothera*
Pulmonaria, 120
    angustifolia, photo, 121
    officinalis 'Sissinghurst White,' 120
    saccharata, 120; photo, 120
Red hot poker, 71-72; photo, 72
Redwood, dawn, 42
Reseda odorata, 131
Rhododendron, 32, 42, 70; photo, 70
Ribbon grass, 119-120; photos, 6, 119
Rockspray cotoneaster, 54-55
Rose bay, 129-130; photos, 32, 130
Rose daphne, 79; photo, 77
Roses, 25, 122
Rudbeckia, photo, 73
    fulgida 'Goldsturm Strain,' 73
Sage, 110-111
    azure, 110; photo, 110
    golden, 35
    Russian, 110; photo, 110
    tricolor, 35
Sago palm, 50-51
Saguaro, 36, 96, 97; photo, 96
St. John's bread, 44
Salix matsudana 'Tortuosa,' 55; photo, 55.
  See also Willow, corkscrew
Salvia officinalis, 110-111
    red, 19
Sand in paths, 28
Santolina
    chamaecyparissus, 111; photo, 111.
      See also Lavender cotton
    incana, 111
Sasa veitchii, 19, 40; photo, 40
Scented plants. See Fragrant plants
Selenicereus, 101, 106-107; photos,
  106, 107
    boeckmannii, 107
    donkelaari, 107
    grandiflorus, 107

hondurensis, 107
    macdonaldiae, 107
    pteranthus, 107
    spinulosis, 107
Senecio
    cineraria, 112; photo, 108. See also
      dusty miller
    x *hybridus*, 63
Serviceberry, 82
Shadowing, 150-151; photo, 150
Shooting star, common, 83
Sidelighting, 151-152; photo, 151
Silhouetting, 151
Silver mound artemisia, 108-109
Silver-foliage plants, 24, 108-112
Sinarundinaria
    murielae, 39
    nitida, 39
Siting the evening garden, 20-21
Snake's-head, 85; photo, 85
Snakeroot, black, 82
Snapdragon, 138
Snow-in-summer, 82
Snow-on-the-mountain, 137-138;
  photo, 137
Snowdrop, 19, 21, 33, 85; photo, 81
Soap tree, 51
Sources, 164-169
Spiraea, 90-91
    prunifolia, 91; photo, 90
    thunbergii, 91
    x *vanhouttei*, 91
    veitchii, 91
Spotlighting, 151
Spruce, blue, 45
Stachys, photo, 145
    byzantina, 145
    lanata, 145
    olympica, 145
Statice, 72
Stewartia koreana, 91; photo, 91
Stock, night-scented, 142-143; photos,
  19, 142
Stone in paths, 26-28
Strawberry tree, 44
Succulents, 40-42
Sundrop, 104
Sunflower, 32
Sunset flowers, 61-67
Sweet alyssum, 17, 20, 81, 88-89
Sweet flag, variegated grassy-leaved, 52
Sweet pea, 128-129; photo, 128
Sweet sultan 'Dairy Maid,' 69-70
Sweet woodruff, 86
Sweetshade, 45
Sweetspire, Virginia, 88
Syringa vulgaris, 131. See also Lilac
Tagetes, 74; photos, 69, 74. See also
  Marigold
    erecta, 74
    'Lemon Gem,' 74
    patula, 74

'Tangerine Gem,' 74
    tenuifolia, 74
Threadleaf coreopsis, 71; photo, 71. See
  also *Coreopsis verticillata* 'Moonbeam'
Thyme, 35
    lemon, 122
Tier lights, 154; photo, 153
Tilia, 131-132
    americana, 132; photo, 131
    cordata, 132
    x *europaea*, 132
    platyphyllos, 132
Tobacco, flowering, 21, 33, 122, 143;
  photos, 123, 143. See also *Nicotiana*
Tomato, 35
Torch lily, 71-72; photo, 72
Trellises, 23-24
Tuberose, 20, 122, 123, 144-145;
  photo, 145
Tulipa, 74-76; photo, 75
Tulips, 74-76, 77
Turtlehead, pink, 62-63
Uplighting, 150-151; photo, 149
Variegated-foliage plants, 19, 32, 113-121
    evergreens, 45
Viburnum, 20, 82
Viola odorata, 132; photo, 132
Violet, sweet, 132; photo 132
Virginia sweetspire, 88
Walkways, 26-28
Walls, 23-24
Washingtonia filifera, 50; photo, 50
Water
  in the evening garden, 28-29
  lighting, 154
Waterlily, 35, 144; photos, 16, 144
White flowers, 81-93
White garden plan, 159
White gaura, 86-87; photo, 86
Whitestripe bamboo, dwarf, 120
Willow
  corkscrew, 37, 55; photo, 55
  dragon-claw, 55
Windflower, Greek, 35
Wisteria, 26, 81
Witch alder, dwarf, 84-85; photo, 84
Woodruff, sweet, 86
Yellow archangel, 118; photo, 118
Yucca, 33, 37
    elata, 51
    filamentosa, 51-52; photo, 51
Zaluzianskya capensis, 107
Zantedeschia aethiopica, 91-93; photos,
  11, 91, 92-93
Zinnia
    angustifolia, 76; photo, 76
    linearis, 76
Zone map, 170-171